Unveiling Mysteries of the Bible

Dr. Grant R. Jeffrey

Frontier Research Publications, Inc.
P.O. Box 129, Station "U", Toronto, Ontario M8Z 5M4

Unveiling Mysteries of the Bible

© Copyright 2002 by Grant R. Jeffrey

All rights reserved. No portion of this book may be reproduced in any form, except for brief quotations in reviews, without the written permission of the publisher.

Library of Congress Cataloging in Publication Data:
Jeffrey, Grant R.
Unveiling Mysteries of the Bible
1. Apologetics   2. Eschatology   3. Bible Science
1. Title

September 2002, Frontier Research Publications, Inc.

ISBN 0-921714-72-6

Second Printing: December 2002

Scripture quotations are from the Authorized King James Version (KJV).

Cover design: The Riordon Design Group Inc.
Printed in Canada: Harmony Printing Limited

"Grant Jeffrey has written an extraordinary new book, *The Signature of God*, that provides astonishing proof that the Bible was inspired by God. Grant is recognized as the leading researcher in Bible Prophecy today."

Hal Lindsey, Hal Lindsey Ministries

"The *Prophecy Study Bible* is a phenomenal publishing effort by one of America's premier prophecy experts. Comprehensive, understandable, and powerful. A great work!" *Dr. Ed Hindsen, Editor – Jesus Study Bible*

"The *Prophecy Study Bible* is the most comprehensive, contemporary, and in-depth study of the most relevant prophecies in the Bible — A must addition to every serious student of the Word of God."

Dr. Chuck Missler – Koinonia House Ministries

"*Prince of Darkness* was written by acclaimed Bible Prophecy teacher Grant R. Jeffrey. This unequaled masterpiece is the result of 30 years of intense research. It will stir you and inspire you as few books have. . . . It is extremely well written — extraordinarily researched and fascinatingly presented . . . this is the best book I have ever read on this subject." *Jack Van Impe, Jack Van Impe Ministries*

"*Armageddon: Appointment With Destiny* has been our hottest single religious title. . . . We took it on with tremendous enthusiasm because there was something very exciting about the way Grant wrote, and it was something that we thought might go beyond the traditional religious audience." *Lou Arnonica, Vice President,*
Bantam Books, New York Times, October 22, 1990

"We are excited about Grant Jeffrey's new book. . . . Now the book with the latest information on prophetic fulfilment, the book of the nineties, is *Armageddon: Appointment With Destiny*. It will show that God is in control and, most importantly, it will also prove to be a powerful witnessing tool to those who need Christ." *David Mainse: Host, 100 Huntley Street*

Table of Contents

Acknowledgements

Unveiling Mysteries of the Bible is an exploration of the many mysterious and puzzling passages found in the Word of God that have perplexed millions of readers of the Bible over the years. This book attempts to answer the questions raised by many people who have never found a satisfactory answer to the questions that have troubled them.

For the last four decades I have accumulated thousands of books dealing with archeology, biblical customs, theology, and history that have provided tremendous material to assist me in finding answers to those questions that have troubled so many readers. During the last few decades, I completed several research trips to the Middle East and Europe. In addition I communicated with bookstores throughout the world acquiring numerous old and often rare books written by great men of God who were diligent students of the Word of God. These volumes contain tremendous archeological, historical and scientific evidence that provide many well reasoned answers to the questions that occur to anyone who studies the Word of God. I am indebted to the work of countless Bible scholars who have previously studied to find the answers to these intriguing questions about many of the most mysterious passages found in the pages of the Holy Scriptures. The Internet and major lending libraries have provided invaluable assistance in completing the research that answers many of the most difficult questions about the Word of God.

This book is the result of almost forty years of research involving the reading of literally thousands of books, Bible commentaries, and countless hours of detailed study of the Scriptures. My parents, Lyle and Florence Jeffrey, have inspired me to pursue a lifelong commitment to the study of the Bible. Their profound love and service to Jesus Christ was motivated by their love of God and a dedication to the command of Jesus "to go into all the world to preach the Gospel." Special thanks to my editorial assistant, Adrienne Jeffrey Tigchelaar, whose excellent editorial services have provided invaluable assistance. My editor Rick Blanchette has provided excellent assistance to produce a readable and well documented manuscript.

I dedicate *Unveiling Mysteries of the Bible* to Kaye, my loving wife and partner in ministry. She continues to inspire my research and writing as well as being my faithful partner in the ministry of Frontier Research Publications, Inc. Without her encouragement and constant assistance this book would never have been completed. I trust that the research revealed in the following pages will inform, inspire, and encourage you to personally study the Bible. If this book renews in the hearts of my readers a new love and appreciation for the Word of God, I will be well rewarded.

Dr. Grant R. Jeffrey
Toronto, Ontario
September, 2002

INTRODUCTION

Unveiling Mysteries of the Bible

Have you ever been puzzled by a mystery in the Bible and you were unable to find anyone who could give you an answer? As a young Christian, I often found myself perplexed by numerous passages in the Scriptures that are difficult to fully understand. I would ask pastors and Bible teachers many questions about these mysteries that fascinated me, including: Where was the Garden of Eden? Where did Cain get his wife? Why do we worship on Sunday? Who were the giants and the sons of God? How can we explain the remarkable miracles during the Exodus? Jesus' virgin birth? The "three days and three nights" and Christ's resurrection? The Star of Bethlehem? The Tower of Babel and the rebuilding of Babylon? I seldom received explanations that satisfied my curiosity.

As I grew in my Christian faith, I began to acquire a large library of books on archeology, theology, and prophecy that provided some of the answers I sought. Over the last four decades I have accumulated a great deal of information and have studied numerous Bible commentaries that began to unveil these fascinating mysteries. This book will explore many of these puzzling passages and offer the best explanation that I have uncovered from personal study. In addition, I have reviewed the works of many of the greatest students of the Word of God. Some of the additional topics covered include: Jonah and the great fish, the darkness at Christ's crucifixion, Joshua's long day, the two genealogies of Jesus, Noah's flood, the lost treasures of the Temple, and the strange account of Saul's encounter with the witch of Endor.

The Bible is certainly the most mysterious book ever written. From Genesis to Revelation, the Scriptures deal with man's quest for meaning and God's mysterious plan to redeem a spiritually lost humanity through His Son, Jesus Christ. The biblical term "mystery" refers to "a secret of the Lord." However, the mystery is also a secret concerning the Lord Jesus Christ that will be revealed to the faithful who seek His divine wisdom. The apostle Paul refers to this mystery concerning Christ Himself, the very Word of God, "the mystery of God, and of the Father, and of Christ; in whom are hid all the treasures of wisdom and knowledge" (Colossians 2:2–3).

For thousands of years, countless generations of Jews and Christians have loved the mysterious passages of the Word of God and have sought to understand their true meaning. Early in the 1900s, Bishop William Thomas Manning wrote about the supreme importance of mystery in God's revelation, "Religion without mystery ceases to be religion."

The Word of God reveals that these hidden mysteries will be revealed to those faithful servants who study its pages. God promises, "The secret things belong unto the Lord our God: but those things which are revealed belong unto us and to our children for ever, that we may do all the words of this law" (Deuteronomy 29:29). The wisest man on earth, King Solomon, who asked God for wisdom and understanding, encouraged us to search out the mysteries of God. "It is the glory of God to conceal a thing: but the honour of kings is to search out a matter" (Proverbs 25:2).

Biblical mysteries challenge our faith as well as our intellect.

Tragically, some have lost their faith in the Word of God because they could not find reasonable explanations for many of these mysterious and strange events. While billions of people have placed their complete faith in Jesus Christ and the Word of God, there are millions who have been intellectually and spiritually frustrated by the fact that they have never found a reasonable explanation for some of the mysteries they encountered in the Word of God.

The illustrations, maps, and photos are placed in many of these chapters to assist you to fully appreciate these remarkable biblical events that have exercised such a compelling power on the minds of people for thousands of years. It is my hope that you will find this book a welcome addition to your home library and that it will be a useful tool in helping you and your family to more fully understand God's wonderful revelation to humanity: the Holy Scriptures.

The final chapter of this book examines the mystery of salvation through the death and resurrection of Jesus Christ. The apostle Paul wrote about the mystery of God's promise of resurrection to eternal life to those who place their faith in Christ's offer of salvation for those who follow Him. "Behold, I shew you a mystery; We shall not all sleep, but we shall all be changed, in a moment, in the twinkling of an eye, at the last trump: for the trumpet shall sound, and the dead shall be raised incorruptible, and we shall be changed" (1 Corinthians 15: 51–52). The final mystery is Christ's promise of our resurrection to an eternal life in heaven. Jesus Christ's own resurrection from the grave is the proof that all who place their faith in Him will also be resurrected at the last day.

I encourage you to join me on a voyage of discovery as we unveil some of the most fascinating mysteries of the Bible.

Notes

1. William Thomas Manning, *Vital Sermons: Model Addresses for Study* Ed. Grenville Kleiser New York: Funk and Wagnalls, 1935.

1

The
Garden of Eden

The first great mystery that confronts the reader of the Bible after reading the account of God's creation of the heavens and the earth is the location of the Garden of Eden. The book of Genesis states, "The Lord God planted a garden eastward in Eden; and there he put the man whom he had formed" (Genesis 2:8). The prophet Ezekiel refers to humanity's first home as "Eden the garden of God" (Ezekiel 28:13). Where was this paradise known as the Garden of Eden actually located? Are there any geographic indications today that allow us to find the location of this ancient paradise of God–man's first home?

The Bible begins its inspired revelation to us by recounting how God created Adam and Eve and gave them a glorious paradise called the Garden of Eden as their home. The Garden of Eden contained everything that humanity needed both to survive and to prosper. In a world without violence, our first parents were commanded to tend the Garden and enjoy the generous bounty that a benevolent Creator had prepared for

His children. Luxurious foliage, figs, and fruit trees made the garden a wonderful home for every manner of creature, including "cattle," "the fowl of the air," and "every beast of the field" (Genesis 2:19–20). God gave Adam a purposeful existence when the Lord "put him into the garden of Eden to dress it and to keep it" (Genesis 2:15). Then, recognizing Adam's need for a companion, God created his wife Eve from a rib from Adam's side.

The Hebrew word translated as "Eden" may be derived from the Sumerian word for "plain" or "steppe." The Greek Septuagint translation that was read in the days of Christ translated "Eden" as the "Garden of Delight," and this led to the association of Eden with Paradise. Some writers in the last few centuries have suggested that the Garden of Eden was only a myth. Some rabbis writing in the mystical Jewish book *Zohar* wrote, "Eden is situated in the seventh heaven and paradise is situated on earth directly opposite to it."[1] However, the precise geographical language and details found in the book of Genesis reveal that its account of Paradise is both realistic and historical. This language strongly supports the conservative position that the Genesis account of the Garden of Eden is a true historical account of what occurred during the earliest days of mankind.

Garden of Eden. Painting by John Martin.

And the Lord God planted a garden eastward in Eden; and there he put the man whom he had formed. And out of the ground made the Lord God to grow every tree that is pleasant to the sight, and good for food; the tree of life also in the midst of the garden, and the tree of knowledge of good and evil. And a river went out of Eden to water the garden; and from thence it was parted, and became into four heads. The name of the first is Pison: that is it which compasseth the whole land of Havilah, where there is gold; And the gold of that land is good: there is bdellium and the onyx stone. And the name of the second river is Gihon: the same is it that compasseth the whole land of Ethiopia. And the name of the third river is Hiddekel: that is it which goeth toward the east of Assyria. And the fourth river is Euphrates. And the Lord God took the man, and put him into the garden of Eden to dress it and to keep it. (Genesis 2:8–15)

There are several theories regarding the possible location of the ancient Garden of Eden. Significantly, Moses recorded that the garden was "eastward" in these words: "the Lord God planted a garden eastward in Eden," (Genesis 2:8). The language in Genesis suggests that the "garden" was located in the territory of "Eden" so the area of Eden could be much larger than the actual Garden of Eden described in Genesis.

The correct identity and present location of each of the four rivers mentioned in the Genesis passage above is vital to any serious attempt to determine the geographical location of the ancient Garden of Eden. The river "Euphrates" is obviously some branch of that great river, while the "Hiddekel" must be the Tigris River that also flows through Iraq, near the ancient city of Babylon. In the book of Daniel the prophet wrote, "I was by the side of the great river, which is Hiddekel" (Daniel 10:4); that is a definite reference to the Tigris. The identification of the other two rivers, the Pishon and the Gihon, presents the greatest difficulty in arriving at a definite location for the Garden of Eden.

The first and greatest problem in solving the mystery of

the Garden of Eden is that the Bible reports a global flood occurred in the days of Noah. This worldwide flood would have produced massive geological change, including the lifting of mountains, and the tremendous destructive effect of the floodwaters would have transformed many geographical features such as ancient riverbeds. The global cataclysm of a worldwide flood covered the whole plain of Mesopotamia with enormous layers of sedimentary rock as deposits from the receding waters. The original rivers and riverbeds called Pishon, Gihon, Hiddekel, and Euphrates would naturally have been covered with these layers of sediment. Therefore, a question that needs to be addressed is this: Are the present-day rivers called Tigris and Euphrates located in the exact area of the ancient rivers mentioned in Genesis? If we assume that God inspired Moses (writing after the Flood) to record the account of Eden using the names of the pre-Flood rivers of Euphrates, et cetera, and because the post-Flood rivers were located in the same area, then the identification of Eden is possible. To add to the difficulty, thousands of years of ice ages and erosion have also created many changes in the landscape. The good news is that major geographical features such as massive riverbeds tend to survive the transient effects of normal erosion. It is possible

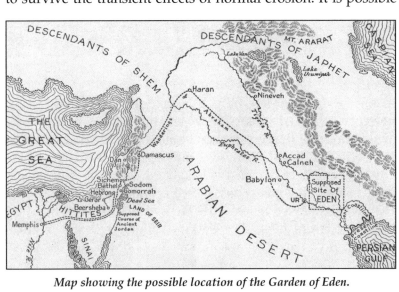

Map showing the possible location of the Garden of Eden.

that a major riverbed would still exist after the worldwide Flood of Noah.

The Northern Theory

The northern theory places Eden in the eastern mountains of Turkey, near the headwaters of the Euphrates and Tigris rivers. The Genesis account notes that "a river went out of Eden to water the garden; and from thence it was parted, and became into four heads" (Genesis 2:10). This passage suggests that there are four headwaters or the beginnings of four rivers, that flow out of one initial river. The locations of the headwaters of both the Euphrates and Tigris in the eastern mountains of Turkey strongly suggests that this is the correct location. This theory is probably the most popular one held by Bible scholars today.

On January 11, 2001, a fascinating article appeared in the *National Post*, one of Canada's largest newspapers.[2] It reported on the research of Michael Sanders, the director of expeditions for a group known as the Mysteries of the Bible Research Foundation, located in Irvine, California. Sanders claimed he had discovered the true site of Eden in the eastern mountains of Turkey. Following his lengthy study of photographs taken by powerful instruments in the satellites operated by the National Aeronautics and Space Administration (NASA), Sanders claimed that he could identify the ancient locations of the four great rivers provided by the description of the Garden of Eden given in the book of Genesis. Sander's conclusion was that the Pishon was the Murat River; the Gihon was the Tigris River; the Hiddekel is the main Euphrates River; and the fourth river, named Euphrates in Genesis, is the present day north fork of the Euphrates river system.

One of the strongest advantages in favor of this northern theory that proposes the mountains of eastern Turkey as the location of Eden is that the headwaters of rivers are found in mountains, not in the low plains such as those that exist through-out most of Iraq, leading south to the Persian Gulf. While it is certainly possible that in the period prior to the Flood the area of the Persian Gulf was much higher than surrounding territories, the existing geography provides compelling evidence in favor of the northern theory.

The Southern Theory

Other writers, including D. J. Hamblin, have concluded that the southern end of the Euphrates and Tigris rivers is the correct location of Eden. D. J. Hamblin, in his book *Has the Garden of Eden Been Located at Last?*[3] concluded that the Garden of Eden was located under the present-day waters of the Persian Gulf near the place where the Tigris and Euphrates rivers finally join together for approximately 120 miles in the Shatt al Arab, "Rivers of the Arabs," that runs through a marsh delta and empty their waters into the Persian Gulf.

Another archaeologist, Juris Zarins, has come to a slightly different conclusion known as the Sumerian theory, as a result of his years of research especially involving the geology of the Arabian Peninsula. He studied the detailed images of the topography of the Middle East as revealed in the photos taken by the LANDSAT satellites orbiting 580 miles above the earth. Zarins' complex theory ultimately suggests that the Gihon River described in Genesis 2:13 is presently known as the Karun River in Iran. He believes that the Pishon is to be found in the ancient Wadi Batin and Wadi Riniah; these are now dry, but LANDSAT satellite images have revealed that this was a major drainage river system of the Arabian Peninsula in the distant past. In confirmation of this identification of Pishon with the ancient river system of the northern Arabian Peninsula, Zarins points to the fact that the aromatic resin bdellium, mentioned in Genesis 2:11, is found there together with ancient gold deposits. Zarins' theory proposes that the Garden of Eden was located under the present-day waters of the Persian Gulf, but that the major area of Eden considered the paradise of Eden by the Sumerian people was located a little further to the south, along the southern shore of the Persian Gulf, and was known in ancient times as *Dilmun*.

Babylonian Theory

Other writers, including the theologian John Calvin, suggested that the Garden of Eden was located in the area of Mesopotamia, near the ancient city of Babylon between the present-day Tigris and Euphrates rivers.[4] The fact that the Tigris and Euphrates rivers join at the Shatt al Arab and run together for over a hundred miles toward the Persian Gulf reminds some writers of the Bible's description that "a river went out of Eden to water the garden; and from thence it was parted, and became into four heads" (Genesis 2:10). Meanwhile, other writers have claimed the evidence suggests that the area far north of Mesopotamia, in the mountainous nation of Armenia, is the proper location.

Theory that Eden Extended from Egypt to India

Some writers, such as the Jewish historian Flavius Josephus, have taken a very extensive view of the size of the Garden of Eden. Josephus wrote about the location of Eden extending from Egypt to India:

> Now the garden was watered by one river, which ran round about the whole earth, and was parted into four parts. And Phison, which denotes a multitude, running into India, makes its exit into the sea, and is by the Greeks called Ganges. Euphrates also, as well as Tigris, goes down into the Red Sea. Now the name Euphrates, or Phrath, denotes either a dispersion, or a flower: by Tiris, or Diglath, is signified what is swift, with narrowness; and Geon runs through Egypt, and denotes what arises from the east, which the Greeks call Nile.[5]

Although the Garden of Eden was large, the Bible does not indicate its actual size. While the Euphrates and Tigris rivers in Mesopotamia are clearly indicated, writers such as Josephus suggest that the reference to the Pishon refers to the great Indus River of India while the Gihon refers to the Nile River of Egypt. If this theory is correct, then the Garden of Eden would extend to cover the entire Middle East land bridge linking the continents of Europe, Africa, and Asia—the Fertile Crescent that gave birth to most of human civilization in the ancient past.

Has the Paradise of Eden Been Found?

Perhaps the most interesting theory that has been presented to date is a new contribution by a noted archeologist from University College, London, Dr. David Rohl, who now claims to have discovered the original paradise of Eden in an extraordinarily beautiful alpine valley in northern Iran. According to an article entitled "Paradise Found" in *The Jerusalem Report*, published February 1, 1999, the beautiful valley has terraced orchards covering its slopes with many kinds of trees laden with fruit.

Dr. Rohl was first led to consider this location when he learned in the 1980s about an ancient Sumerian cuneiform clay tablet inscription called "Enmerkar and the Lord of Aratta" located in the Museum of the Orient in Istanbul, Turkey. This ancient inscription described a five-thousand-year-old route leading to "Eden" that took the emissary on a three-month journey through seven passes leading through the Zagros Mountains to the edge of Mount Sahand. Naturally, Rohl was motivated to follow this curious lead. After years of research, Rohl hired a guide and traveled north toward Kurdistan, one of the most dangerous areas of the Middle East. Rohl concluded that the Gihon and Pishon Rivers described in Genesis 2:11–13 are the present-day Araxes and Uizhun Rivers. The area has many ancient gold mines, and the local inhabitants know the Uizhun River as the "Golden River." Rohl is returning to Iran to attempt further research regarding the mystery of Eden. It is noteworthy that Rohl has upheld the reliability of the Bible as a reliable historical document: "I consider the Bible a historical document just like the writings of Herodotus or a text of Rameses II."[6] A full account of Rohl's fascinating discoveries appears in his book *Legend: The Genesis of Civilization*.[7]

Conclusion

At this time we must admit that it is impossible to dogmatically assert that we have located the Garden of Eden geographically. However, since this account concerning the creation of Adam and Eve is so important to our understanding of God's unfolding plan for humanity, it is worthwhile to continue research that may someday provide the answer to one of the Bible's great mysteries.

Notes

1. *Zohar* I, p. 125a.
2. Peter Goodspeed, "Garden of Eden in Turkey, says Bible scholar," *National Post*, 11 January, 2001.
3. D. J. Hamblin, *Has the Garden of Eden Been Located at Last?*, 22 January 2001.
4. H. Lockyer, ed., *Nelson's Illustrated Bible Dictionary*, Nashville: Thomas Nelson, 1986, pp.318–320.
5. Flavius Josephus, *Antiquities of the Jews*, Book I, chapter I.
6. "Paradise Found," *The Jerusalem Report*, 1 February, 1999.
7. David Rohl, Legend: *The Genesis of Civilization*, London: Century, Random House, 1998.

2

The Mystery of Where Cain Found a Wife

One of the mysteries of the Bible that has troubled millions of Christians over the centuries concerns the question of where Adam's son, Cain, found his wife. The Scriptures record that the only two humans specially created by God were Adam and Eve, the first parents of the human race. All other people were born naturally to their human mother. Therefore, it is logical and inescapable that Cain and his brothers had no other option than to marry their sisters, by necessity, if they were to carry on the human race as commanded by God. Following Cain's murder of his brother Abel, the Bible declares that Adam and Eve had another son named Seth many years later. It is probable that Eve gave birth to other unnamed daughters and sons both before and after the birth of Seth.

Adam and Eve had other sons and daughters throughout their very long lives. "And Adam lived an hundred and thirty years, and begat a son in his own likeness, after his image; and called his name Seth: And the days of Adam after he had begotten Seth were eight hundred years: and he begat sons and daughters" (Genesis 5:3–4). Many people naturally wonder how Cain could have married his sister, since the Law of God as recorded in the Bible clearly prohibits anyone from marrying a close family relation such as a sister, mother, aunt, or niece.

God commanded Moses to record His laws for the Children of Israel: Moses wrote, "None of you shall approach to any that is near of kin to him, to uncover their nakedness: I am the Lord. . . . The nakedness of thy sister, the daughter of thy father, or daughter of thy mother, whether she be born at home, or born abroad, even their nakedness thou shalt not uncover" (Leviticus 18:6, 9).

However, it is important to recognize that God did not proclaim these laws against incest until thousands of years after the lives of Adam and Eve. Therefore, when Cain and his brothers married their sisters there was no breaking of God's law. Furthermore, the Scriptures record that God specifically commanded Adam and his children to "multiply and replenish the earth." Moses recorded the Lord's divine command to Adam's descendents as follows: "And God blessed them, and God said unto them, Be fruitful, and multiply, and replenish the earth, and subdue it: and have dominion over the fish of the sea, and over the fowl of the air, and over every living thing that moveth upon the earth" (Genesis 1:28). Therefore, Cain's marriage to his sister was in obedience to God's command.

In addition, since there were no other non-related women for them to marry, it was a logical necessity for Cain and his brothers to marry their sisters if humanity was to survive in accordance with God's command to "multiply and replenish the earth" (Genesis 1:28). If Cain and his brothers refused to marry their sisters, then humanity would have quickly become extinct. However, as soon as the human population had expanded during the third generation and following to the extent that it was no longer necessary to marry one's sister, the very natural instinct to search out a non-relative as a mate took over.

Another issue that has been raised by critics is the problem of possible birth defects that might occur when siblings marry and produce children. Genetic defects are likely to multiply and produce deformities in their offspring when siblings mate together because defective recessive genes in the DNA of siblings will combine to produce birth defects. However, it is important to recognize that there were no genetic defects in the DNA of Adam's children during the first few generations following the creation of Adam and Eve. Many generations later, after the sinful fall of Adam and Eve, genetic defects in the DNA of their descendents would gradually accumulate. This would eventually lead to birth defects in the offspring of sibling marriages when genetic defects in the similar DNA of a brother and sister combined to increase the probability of giving birth to a child with a tragic mutation. However, by that time the natural taboo against sibling marriage and the opportunity to find non-related wives facilitated the natural inclination to seek mates from other families.

History reveals that growing awareness of the genetic risks arising from the combining of defective DNA when brothers and sisters marry is the reason that virtually all societies throughout history have developed powerful taboos and restrictions against incest. In addition, most societies have created legislation forbidding marriages between close relatives, similar to those restrictions recorded in the Bible.

3

The Sons of God and the Giants

One of the strangest biblical mysteries is found in the pages of the book of Genesis regarding the mysterious account about the "sons of God" and their sexual relations with the "daughters of men," producing the "giants" that were born to them in those ancient days. Many have wondered if these "sons of God" could actually be fallen angels. Many translations use the word "angels" in this passage instead of the "sons of God."

The term "sons of God" as found in Genesis 6:2,4 is also used in five other passages in the Old Testament. Every single time the expression refers to angels. In Job 1:6 and 2:1, this term "sons of God" clearly refers to angels. Daniel 3:25 describes the fourth "man" who appeared among the three Jewish heroes — Shadrach, Meshach, and Abednego — in the fiery furnace. He appeared as "the Son of Man" and obviously supernaturally saved these heros from certain death.

Many of the Jewish commentaries on the Torah concluded that the expression "sons of God" in Genesis 6 refers to fallen angels. In the first few centuries following the life of Jesus Christ, several early Church writers wrote about these "sons of God." The well respected Christian writer Justin Martyr wrote, "But the angels transgressed . . . were captivated by the love of women, and begat children."[1] The apostle Peter in his Second Epistle reports, "For if God spared not the angels that sinned, but cast them down to hell, and delivered them into chains of darkness, to be reserved unto judgment; and spared not the old world, but saved Noah the eighth person, a preacher of righteousness, bringing in the flood upon the world of the ungodly" (2 Peter 2:4–5).

Genesis 6 recounts how the "sons of God," the fallen angels, were a key reason God was forced to destroy the earth with a great flood during the days of Noah. The Scriptures reveal that a large number of angels joined in Satan's initial rebellion against God in the dateless past. Among those fallen angels known as "the sons of God" who rebelled against God were a number who chose also to violate God's law forbidding sexual relations with humanity. The book of Genesis records, "The sons of God saw the daughters of men that they were fair; and they took them wives of all which they chose" (Genesis 6:2). This angelic disobedience was an abomination to God. He determined then to destroy the mutant hybrid offspring of this unholy union of angels and men that included the whole of humanity, save for Noah and his family.

However, God mercifully promised Noah's generation that He would delay His prophesied judgment for "one hundred and twenty years," in which He gave humanity an opportunity to repent. During the next 120 years, Noah preached righteousness to his wicked and violent generation. However, the totality of that generation rejected Noah's call for repentance and mocked Noah as he built the ark to save his family and those animals that God commanded him to take on board.

The Bible describes Noah as "a just man and perfect in his generations, and Noah walked with God" (Genesis 6:9). We know that no human can be spiritually perfect. What does the Bible mean in this passage when it describes Noah as "perfect in his generations"? This curious expression appears to refer to the fact that Noah and his family were still perfect in their reproductive history. As a result of the unholy union of these fallen angels with sinful humanity, virtually all of humanity's families had become demonically infected by this satanic infestation through the corruption of the seed from "the sons of God" (the fallen angels) by the time of the Flood. It appears that the last remaining family that had not succumbed to this tragic demonic infestation was the family of Noah, a man "perfect in his generations." The Epistle of Peter describes Noah as a "preacher of righteousness." Peter wrote that God, "spared not the old world, but saved Noah the eighth person, a preacher of righteousness, bringing in the flood upon the world of the ungodly." (2 Peter 2:5).

Satan's apparent purpose in directing this demonic corruption of humanity through the fallen "sons of God" was intended to prevent any pure, undefiled genetic human line through which the promised Messiah, Jesus Christ, humanity's only hope of salvation, could be born. If Satan had been successful in this attempt to demonize all humanity, salvation through the prophesied Messiah would have been impossible. Jesus the Messiah could not, as holy God, be born to a human mother whose ancestors had been defiled by demons.

Genesis 6:4 describes, "There were giants on the earth in those days; and also after that, when the sons of God came in unto the daughters of men, and they bare children to them, the same became mighty men which were of old, men of renown." It is likely that the genetic offspring of the "sons of God" (these fallen angels) led to the "demigods" reported in Greek literature and many other legends of ancient history regarding "gods" descending to earth and having intercourse with humans. Genesis 6:4 declares, "There were giants in the earth in those days; and also after that." This passage reveals that Satan tried a second time to demonize humanity after the Flood. The phrase "and also after that" shows that after the Flood, Satan must have directed some fallen angels to once again try to mate with women to prevent the possibility of the birth of the Messiah.

The descendants born to these "sons of God" (fallen angels) through alliances with humans after the Flood were those "men of great stature" that the twelve Israeli spies encountered and later warned Moses about. "And there we saw the giants, the sons of Anak, which come of the giants: and we were in our own sight as grasshoppers, and so we were in their sight" (Numbers 13:33). There are numerous references in the Old Testament to the giant races that Israel encountered in their conquest of the Promised Land. The Scriptures reported that centuries later David slew the giant Goliath: "And there went out a champion out of the camp of the Philistines named Goliath, of Gath, whose height was six cubits and a span" (1 Samuel 17:4). One of David's mighty men killed Goliath's giant brother. Some of these giants had six fingers and six toes and were over ten feet tall. "And there was yet a battle in Gath, where was a man of great stature, that had on every hand six fingers, and on every foot six toes, four and twenty in number; and he also was born to the giant" (2 Samuel 21:20). The area of Bashan in Lebanon was known as the ancient land of giants. "For only Og king of Bashan remained of the remnant of giants; behold, his bedstead was a bedstead of iron; is it not in Rabbath of the children of Ammon? nine cubits was the length thereof, and four cubits the breadth of it, after the cubit of a man" (Deuteronomy 3:11).

The Jewish historian Flavius Josephus in his *Antiquities of the Jews*, says, "Many angels of god accompanied with women, and begat sons that proved unjust . . . these men did what resembled the acts of those whom the Grecians called giants." (Book I, chapter 3)[2]. Josephus notes that the bones of these giants were still available for inspection in his day (Book V, chapter 2).[2]

The Bible describes only male angels, and the Hebrew word for angel is masculine. The Scriptures clearly indicate that the fallen angels of Genesis 6 were physically capable of reproduction. If these angels were not biologically male, they could not have produced giants as children from their unholy union with the "daughters of men." Satan cannot create anything; he can only pervert the good creation of God into something sinful. Therefore, God must have created these fallen angels, the "sons of God," originally as male angels with the capability of biological reproduction.

Many Christians, upon reading the account of the Israelites taking possession of the Promised Land, have been troubled by

God's command to annihilate the inhabitants of Canaan. If these people of Canaan were the offspring of demonic angelic-human relations, no wonder God commanded that they be wiped out. There are many Scriptures that show that these people were not normal humans (Numbers 13:32–33; Deuteronomy 2:10, 20).

The Canaanites and other pagan tribes in Canaan indulged in terrible idolatry and gruesome pagan practices, such as offering their firstborn sons as burnt sacrifices before their idol Moloch. They engaged in temple prostitution and sexual perversion of every kind. God knew that Satan's plan was to tempt the Jews into paganism, to infiltrate and defile the Chosen People. Israel's failure to remove the people of Canaan from the Promised Land as God commanded caused Israel enormous temptations and distractions for the next thousand years. It appears as if these pagan races inhabiting the Promised Land were demonically infected races who were already given over to Satan.

This demonic condition of the pagan races confronting Israel provides a possible answer to the mystery of why God commanded the Israelites to utterly destroy these races before they possessed the land of Canaan. If this conclusion is correct, then God's command to destroy these races was in fact a severe mercy, similar to the destruction of a depraved humanity in the Flood, that prevented Satan from hindering the salvation of humanity by destroying Noah and his family, the ancestors of Jesus the Messiah.

Revelation 20:1–3 tells us that after the Battle of Armageddon an angel of God will bind Satan with a chain and consign him to "the bottomless pit" for a thousand years until he is cast forever into the lake of fire. The fallen angels, "the sons of God" that rebelled against God at the beginning of human history, will finally be judged by God at the Great White Throne Judgment at the end of the Millennium. "And the angels which kept not their first estate, but left their own habitation, he hath reserved in everlasting chains under darkness unto the judgment of the great day" (Jude 6).

Notes

1. Justin Martyr, *The Second Apology of Justin for the Christians*, Ante-Nicene Fathers (Edinborough: 1890).
2. Flavius Josephus, *Antiquites of the Jews*. transl.

4

The Tower of Babel

The story of the Tower of Babel and the supernatural confusion of all human languages as a result of man's rebellion against God remains one of the most intriguing mysteries in the Word of God. To the astonishment of many Bible critics, this fascinating account has actually been confirmed through the discoveries of archeologists in ancient Iraq.

The Bible declares that from the beginning of mankind, the creation of Adam and Eve, humanity had only one language. "And the whole earth was of one language, and of one speech" (Genesis 11:1). This unity of language existed until the dispersion of the human population, following the supernatural confusion of their language after man's rebellion against God at the Tower of Babel. The Bible records that the Lord purposely confounded the language of all the people on earth (Genesis 11:9) so they could not understand the speech of their neighbors. This inability to understand each other's communications forced them to abandon their Tower of Babel and disperse throughout the earth.

The Bible's Account of the Tower of Babel

And it came to pass, as they journeyed from the east, that they found a plain in the land of Shinar; and they dwelt there. And they said one to another, Go to, let us make brick, and burn them thoroughly. And they had brick for stone, and slime [asphalt] had they for morter. And they said, Go to, let us build us a city and a tower, whose top may reach unto heaven; and let us make us a name, lest we be scattered abroad upon the face of the whole earth. And the Lord came down to see the city and the tower, which the children of men builded. And the Lord said, Behold, the people is one, and they have all one language; and this they begin to do: and now nothing will be restrained from them, which they have imagined to do. Go to, let us go down, and there confound their language, that they may not understand one another's speech. So the Lord scattered them abroad from thence upon the face of all the earth: and they left off to build the city. (Genesis 11:2–8)

Babylon and its Three Towers. Painting by William Simpson.

The people had gathered together in sinful pride against God in their attempt to build a tower that would reach to the heavens. Moses recorded God's subsequent judgment and destruction of the Tower of Babel and the city of Babylon. The archeologists discovered that the ancient remains of the Tower of Babel are vitrified (melted to form a kind of rough glass). This fact suggests that God used a huge amount of heat to destroy the Tower of Babel.

Philologists, scientists who study the origin of languages, have concluded that it is probable that the thousands of dialects and languages throughout the planet can be traced back to an original language in man's ancient past. Professor Alfredo Trombetti claims that he can prove that there was a common origin of all languages.[1] Max Mueller, one of the greatest Oriental language scholars, declared that all human languages can be traced back to one single original language.[2]

The French government sent Professor M. Oppert to report on a number of the cuneiform inscriptions discovered in the ruins of ancient Babylon. Professor Oppert translated a long inscription by King Nebuchadnezzar (died 562 B.C.) in which the king referred to the ancient tower in the Chaldean language as *Barzippa*, which means "Tongue-tower." The Greeks used the word *Borsippa*, with the same meaning of "tongue-tower," to describe the ruins of the Tower of Babel. This inscription of King Nebuchadnezzar clearly identified the original tower of Borsippa with the Tower of Babel as described by Moses in the book of Genesis. Nebuchadnezzar was known as a great builder of cities, palaces, and temples to commemorate his pagan gods.

King Nebuchadnezzar's Inscription Found in the Ruins of the Tower of Babel

King Nebuchadnezzar decided to rebuild the base of the ancient Tower of Babel, built over sixteen centuries earlier by the biblical Nimrod, the first King of Babylon, who originally founded the city in the centuries following the Flood. Nebuchadnezzar called the ruined structure "the Temple of the Spheres." During the millennium since God had destroyed it, the tower was reduced from its original huge height and magnificence until only the enormous base of the tower (460 feet by 690 feet), standing some 275 feet high, remained within the outskirts of the city of Babylon.

Today the ruins have been reduced to about 150 feet above the plain with a circumference of 2,300 feet. King Nebuchadnezzar rebuilt the enormous city of Babylon in great magnificence with gold and silver. He then decided to

Tower of Babel. Illustration by Gustave Doré.

rebuild the lowest platform of the Tower of Babel in honor of the Chaldean gods. At great cost, King Nebuchadnezzar resurfaced the base of the Tower of Babel with gold, silver, cedar, and fir on top of a hard surface of baked clay bricks. These bricks were engraved with the seal of King Nebuchadnezzar.

In an inscription found on the base of the ruins of the Tower of Babel, King Nebuchadnezzar spoke in his own words, confirming one of the most fascinating events of the ancient past as recorded in the Word of God:

The tower, the eternal house, which I founded and built.
I have completed its magnificence with silver, gold,
other metals, stone, enamelled bricks, fir and pine.
The first which is the house of the earth's base,
the most ancient monument of Babylon;
I built and finished it.
I have highly exalted its head with bricks covered with copper.
We say for the other, that is, this edifice, the house of the
seven lights of the earth,
the most ancient monument of Borsippa.
A former king built it, (they reckon 42 ages) but he did not
complete its head.
Since a remote time, people had abandoned it,
without order expressing their words.
Since that time the earthquake and the thunder had
dispersed the sun-dried clay.
The bricks of the casing had been split,
and the earth of the interior had been scattered in heaps.
Merodach, the great god, excited my mind to repair this
building.
I did not change the site nor did I take away the foundation.
In a fortunate month, in an auspicious day,
I undertook to build porticoes around the crude brick masses,
and the casing of burnt bricks.
I adapted the circuits, I put the inscription of my name in
the Kitir of the portico.
I set my hand to finish it. And to exalt its head.
As it had been in ancient days, so I exalted its summit.

Professor M. Oppert first translated this amazing inscription into French, and William Loftus later translated it into English in his book *Travels and Researches in Chaldea and Susiana*[3] This remarkable ancient inscription confirms the historical accuracy of one of the most unusual and fascinating stories found in the book of Genesis. The pagan king of Babylon, King Nebuchadnezzar, confirmed in his own words the unusual details that "a former king built it, but he did not complete its head [top]." This ancient inscription confirmed the accuracy of the Genesis account that God had prevented the original builders from completing the top of the Tower of Babel. Most significantly, King Nebuchadnezzar's inscription declares that the reason the original king could not complete the tower was that they could not express their own words: "Since a remote time, people had abandoned it, without order expressing their words." Thus, King Nebuchadnezzar admitted that his ancestors actually lost their ability to "express their words," to control their language and communications!

"A former king built it, but he did not complete its head. Since a remote time, people had abandoned it." Compare these words of King Nebuchadnezzar with the inspired words of Moses in Genesis 11:7: "So the Lord scattered them abroad from thence upon the face of all the earth: and they left off to build the city." Even more startling is the phrase of the pagan king where he declared that the reason they could not complete the top of the "tongue-tower" was that the "people abandoned it, without order expressing their words." This expression by the pagan King Nebuchadnezzar clearly confirms the historical event recorded in Genesis that God supernaturally "confused the language of all the earth" and that He "scattered them abroad from thence upon the face of all the earth" (Genesis 11:2–8). This inscription by King Nebuchadnezzar regarding the supernatural account about the Tower of Babel provides compelling evidence that the Bible gives us a historically accurate record of the unprecedented event described in the book of Genesis.

Notes

1. Alfredo Trombetti, *Elementi di glottologia* Bologna: Regia Accademia delle Scienze dell'Instituto di Bologna, Classe di Scienze Morali (1912-13), Estratta dalla Serie I. Tomo VII.
2. Max Mueller, Internet site: http://www.geocities.com/ indianfascism/fascism/myths_ancient_history.htm.
3. William Kennett Loftus, *Travels and Researches in Chaldea and Susiana* (London: James Nisbet, 1857) 29.

5

Noah's Flood

The Scriptures' account of a worldwide Flood that destroyed virtually all of humanity in the days of Noah is one of the most controversial passages found in the Word of God. The mysteries concerning the Flood provide many problems and difficulties for most readers of the Bible. While there are many scientists who dispute the fact of a global flood, there is enormous evidence throughout the planet that water did cover the surface of the earth at some point in the distant past. The existence of vast areas of sedimentary rocks proves that water once covered these areas. In this chapter we will examine several of the mysterious aspects of this unprecedented event and attempt to answer some of the questions that have puzzled people regarding the global Flood.

How Large was Noah's Ark?

And God said unto Noah . . . Make thee an ark of gopher wood; rooms shalt thou make in the ark, and thou shalt pitch it within and without with pitch. And this is the fashion which thou shalt make it of: The length of the ark shall be three hundred cubits, the breadth of it fifty cubits, and the height of it thirty cubits. A window shalt thou make to the ark, and in a cubit shalt thou finish it above; and the door of the ark shalt thou set in the side therof; with lower, second, and third stories shalt thou make it (Genesis 6:13–16).

Scholars believe the ancient cubit was approximately eighteen inches in length. Given that assumption, the ark would have been 450 feet long, 75 feet wide, and 45 feet high. The ark had three decks with a total floor space of 101,250 square feet. The three decks provided a height equal to a four-story building. Thus, Noah's ark was clearly the largest ocean-going ship ever built until the late nineteenth century. According to shipbuilders, the ark's design was perfect for surviving a yearlong voyage.

Naval architects have noted that the biblical dimensions of Noah's ark are startlingly different from those reported in the ancient mythical account of the flood found in the *Epic of Gilgamesh* inscribed in the Babylonian clay tablets (discussed later in this chapter). The mythical Babylonian account of the ark's dimensions describes a ship that was built in a square shape, with its length and width being 120 cubits (180 feet by 180 feet). It is reported that the Babylonian ark was a minimum of ninety feet in height with nine decks. Any ship builder would realize that such a construction would result in an enormously unwieldy and top-heavy vessel that would simply spin around in response to ocean currents and wind action. Such a mythical vessel would be entirely unseaworthy and likely to founder in violent seas.

The Construction of the Ark

The Bible indicates that Noah constructed the ark under the direct guidance and instructions of God. Noah would have certainly hired additional workers to augment the labor of his family. His neighbors probably thought his plan to build a ship on dry land was insane, since there was no rain before the Flood. However, there is no reason to doubt that they would have been willing to work for hire on Noah's project.

The Bible records that Noah used gopher wood to construct

the ark. Then they used a "pitch" (Hebrew *kaphar*) to cover the outside surface of the ship. This may indicate that a form of asphalt was spread over the ark "within and without" to waterproof its surface so it would withstand a year-long voyage. The Scripture declares that the waters covered the surface of the earth to the extent that the floodwaters extended to fifteen cubits (twenty-two and a half feet) above the highest mountains. "And the waters prevailed exceedingly upon the earth; and all the high hills, that were under the whole heaven, were covered. Fifteen cubits upward did the waters prevail; and the mountains were covered" (Genesis 7:19–20).

This suggests that the Ark had a draft of fifteen cubits. Thus it would have been extremely stable in water. The biblical account does not indicate that the worldwide waters were so deep that they covered our existing high mountains, such as Mount Ararat, which are now 17,000 feet above sea level. Many scientists believe that the mountains that existed before the Flood were much smaller than the huge mountains that exist today. It is quite possible that the enormous geological changes that occurred during the worldwide flood resulted in the rise of the present-day ranges of huge mountains that characterize the globe today.

Naval architects have noted that at 450 feet long and 75 feet wide the length-to-width ratio of Noah's ark was six to one. This particular length-to-width ratio would provide excellent stability for a ship in the face of the severe weather and high waves associated with a worldwide flood. Modern shipbuilders claim that the ark's dimensions (a cross section of 45 feet in height with a beam width of 75 feet together with a length of 450 feet) would make it almost impossible to overturn, despite massive waves and high seas. In consideration of the fact that the ark was unpowered and intended to simply float as an ocean-going barge, its construction was perfectly adapted to survive the severe sea conditions associated with the storms produced by a global flood.

A fascinating experiment was conducted at the famous Scripps Institute of Oceanography at La Jolla, California, testing the seaworthiness of the ark. This experiment using a scale model of the Ark was completed for the documentary *In Search of Noah's Ark* produced by Sun Classics Inc. A mechanical wave generator simulated massive waves greater than any that have ever been observed in the oceans. However, the huge waves were unable to capsize or sink the model ark that was built to the exact scale recorded in the book of Genesis.

Was Noah's Ark Large Enough to Carry the Animals?

The ark was as long as one-and-a-half football fields. A careful analysis of the biblical account reveals that the ark would have possessed an available floor space on the three decks of the ark of over 100,000 square feet. That means that the ark had floor space for animals greater than that of twenty basketball courts. In addition, the total capacity of the ship would have amounted to 1,518,750 cubic feet. To place this enormous volume in perspective, consider that the ark held an amount of storage space equal to that found in approximately 569 modern railroad stock cars. A standard North American railroad stock car with double decks will carry approximately 240 adult sheep. Therefore, the ark could have held as many as 125,000 adult sheep.

Although there are more than a million species found throughout the globe, the vast majority of those species are capable of surviving in the water, including over 21,000 species of fish; over 100,000 mollusks such as clams, oysters, and mussels; and over 30,000 species of tiny single-celled entities known as protozoans. In addition, over 830,000 species of arthropods, including crabs, lobsters, shrimp, and water-borne fleas, as well as 35,000 species of worms plus enormous numbers of insects, would be capable of surviving in the water.

Scholars such as Dr. Henry M. Morse, in his book *The Biblical Basis for Modern Science,* estimate that there are approximately "18,000 species of land animals alive today (that is birds, mammals, reptiles, and amphibians)."[1] With a storage capacity of 1,518,750 cubic feet capable of holding approximately 125,000 sheep-sized animals, it is obvious that the ark could easily have held two of each of 18,000-plus species, or approximately 36,000 individual animals, most of which would be considerably smaller than an adult sheep. There are relatively few very large animal species, such as elephants, giraffes, and cattle, compared to the thousands of very small species including rodents, reptiles, and monkeys. Even relatively large mammals could be accommodated in the ark by the process of God directing Noah to acquire young animals that had not yet achieved full adult size. Even if we enlarge the number of species to 40,000 individuals averaging the size of an adult sheep, the Ark would still have used only one-third of its vast capacity. Numerous species of birds would have survived either in the ark or many could have survived by resting on the enormous amount of debris that undoubtedly floated on the surface of the water.

Could Noah's Ark Hold the Necessary Food?

And take thou unto thee of all food that is eaten, and thou shalt gather it to thee; and it shall be for food for thee, and for them (Genesis 6:21).

Another matter that is often raised is the question of the storage of the necessary food to enable the numerous species to survive for a year. The massive storage capacity of the ark, after allowing one-third (518,750 cubic feet) for animals, still amounted to two-thirds of its total storage space (approximately 1,000,000 cubic feet) for food, water, and living space for Noah's family. This was sufficient to provide for the amount of food that would be needed by both the animals and Noah's family. In addition, it is certainly possible that the passive conditions for animals in the ark greatly minimized the amount of food required. Some have suggested that it is possible that God allowed the animals to minimize their activity and caloric intake in a manner similar to that seen in animals such as bears or squirrels that reduce their activity and minimize their need for food during a winter-long hibernation. Many groups of animals exhibit at least a latent ability to hibernate or become dormant during adverse conditions.

How Were the Animals Gathered into the Ark?

Some writers have suggested that the problem of gathering two specimens of every species of land animal and taking them into the ark was impossible. Some have suggested that virtually all animal species have the ability to sense impending danger, and this may have been used by God to motivate them to move toward a place of safety. However, the Scriptures indicate that God Himself supernaturally gathered the multitude of animals and brought them to Noah's Ark "two and two." The Scriptures recorded, "There went in two and two unto Noah into the ark, the male and the female, as God had commanded Noah" (Genesis 7:9).

Where Did the Water Come From— And Where Did It Go?

The Bible reveals that God opened the canopy of the pre-Flood atmosphere to release huge amounts of water that had encircled the planet since Creation as "the firmament." In addition, Genesis declares that the Lord opened "the fountains of the great deep": "In the six hundredth year of Noah's life, in the second month, the seventeenth day of the month, the same day were all the fountains of the great deep broken up, and the windows of heaven were opened. And the rain was upon the earth forty days and forty nights" (Genesis 7:11–12).

The question of where the waters went when they receded following the end of the Flood is answered by looking at the massive geological changes that occurred during and following the remarkable Flood event recorded in Genesis 6–7. In addition to the rise of great mountain ranges, the earth experienced the creation of enormous depressions and the development of deep valleys in the present-day ocean floors. These great depressions were filled with the waters from the Flood, creating the massive oceans that now cover 70 percent of the globe. To visualize the staggering amount of water that was available to cover the entire earth during Noah's Flood, it is worthwhile to realize that if the sphere of the earth were made as smooth as a basketball, the water in the deep ocean basins is sufficient to cover the entire earth to a depth of two miles (10,000-plus feet).

Any examination of the great river valleys throughout the globe reveals that the present level of the rivers could not possibly account for the huge size of these river valleys. In other words, the geological evidence from far up the mountainsides of these large river valleys and the massive alluvial deposits beneath the riverbeds reveal that the original ancient rivers must have vastly exceeded the present-day streams. There are many areas throughout the world where you can witness the surviving evidence in the form of seashells, fish fossils, etc., far from any existing river, lake, or sea. This fossil evidence reveals that massive seas once covered large portions of North America, as well as many other parts of the globe. In the early 1930s, laborers digging a well near my grandfather's farm in the Ottawa Valley, Ontario, Canada, discovered the fossilized remains of a whale. Another fossilized whale was found in the 1960s on a farm near Frontier Ranch, my family's former Western-style summer children's camp, where I grew up near Arnprior, Ontario.

The Babylonian Story of the Flood and Noah

During a study trip to London several years ago, I examined the copy of the Babylonian Deluge Tablet displayed in the famous British Museum, which holds an enormous collection of archeological discoveries from the Middle East that support the truthfulness of many of the Scriptural accounts of historical events that occurred during biblical times. This ancient Babylonian clay tablet was created more than four millennia ago and contains one of the most important inscriptions from the earliest days of humanity. The Deluge Tablet is the eleventh book of the Chaldean *Epic of Gilgamesh* (dated 2200 B.C.). The person known as Gilgamesh is called Nimrod, the builder of the original city of Babylon, as recorded in Genesis 11. The epic poem, *Epic of Gilgamesh*, recounts the story of the Flood as given to Gilgamesh by an older relative, a man named *Nuh-napishtim*, (also called *Atrahasis*) known as "the very wise or pious." This *Nuh-napishtim* is the Babylonian name for Noah.

The Babylonian *Epic of Gilgamesh* contains a remarkable account of the Flood. It is of great interest to scholars because the Deluge Tablet, the eleventh chapter of the poem, contains startling parallels to the Flood story as found in Genesis. According to the Scriptures, the Flood destroyed almost all animals and virtually the whole of the human race, save for Noah and his family. Such a devastating global event would certainly leave a profound mark on the collective memory of humanity. If such a global catastrophe actually happened, there would inevitably be a universal memory of the Flood that would show up in the ancient histories and literature of all ancient cultures. Scholars have discovered a significant number of remarkable Flood stories in the histories of almost every single race throughout every inhabited continent. Professor James George Frazer recounted in his book *Folk-lore in the Old Testament* numerous Flood accounts as found in Babylon, Persia, Greece, India, China, Australia, Polynesia, North and South America, Europe, and Africa that display an astonishing number of parallels with the biblical account.[2] While these non-biblical accounts contain a number of variations from the Genesis account, the discovery of numerous key points in these stories that parallel the Flood story provide compelling evidence that this unique global event truly occurred as recorded in the Bible.

The Babylonian Deluge Tablet and the Biblical Flood Account

The Deluge Tablet describes the flood as a punishment of the "gods" in response to man's sin as described in Genesis. The "gods" sent a flood to punish humanity's sins and terrible

The Deluge Tablet from the Babylonian Epic of Gilgamesh.

violence similar to the biblical account ("the city was full of violence"). It is interesting to note that both accounts claim that Noah and his family departed from the ark in the general area of Mount Ararat (Turkey). The Babylonian Atrahasis (Noah) was commanded to build a ship for his family (plus the ship builders) and a variety of animals, as well as food. The ship (ark) was built with a deck house or covering and was covered with bitumen (pitch) both inside and outside, as Genesis described ("within and without"). In the Babylonian epic the rain lasted only six days and nights, as opposed to the "forty days and forty nights" as found in the biblical account. In both stories several birds are sent out in succession (including a raven and a dove) to determine the conditions outside the ark. Interestingly, both accounts state that the final bird sent out from the Ark failed to return, suggesting that a safe harbor was located. Both accounts report that the ark finally rested on a mountaintop and the grateful survivors exited the ark to offer thanksgiving sacrifices to God. In both accounts God (or the gods) promise that humanity will never again be punished by a flood. The Deluge Tablet claims that Atrahasis (Noah) and his wife started rebuilding the race in a restored country in Mesopotamia exactly as recorded in Genesis.[3]

Portions of the Deluge Tablet in the Epic of Nimrod
(Haupt, Nimrod-Efos, No. 70.)

Nuh-napishtim (Noah) saith to him, even to Gilgamesh;
Let me unfold to thee, Gilgamesh, a secret story,
And the decree of the gods let me tell thee
Shurippak, a city thou knowest, On the bank of Euphrates it
    lieth;
That city was full of violence, and the gods within it,
To make a flood their heart urged them, even the mighty gods.

Man of Shurippak, son of Ubara-Tutu,
Pull down the house, build a ship.
Leave goods, seek life. Property forsake, and life preserve.
Cause seed of life of every sort to go up into the ship.
The ship which thou shalt build. . . .

I will [go] down to the Ocean, [and] with my, [Lord] will I
    dwell
[Upon] you it will rain heavily. . . .
I laid down its form, I figured (or fashioned) it:
I chose a mast (or rudder-pole), and supplied what was neces-
    sary:
Six sars of bitumen I poured over the outside,
Three sars of bitumen [I poured over] the inside. . . .

With all that I had of seed of life of every sort [I freighted it] . . .
I put on board all my family and my clan;
Cattle of the field, wild beasts of the field,
all the craftsmen, I put on board. . . .

When the Lord of Storm at even tide causeth the heavens to rain
    heavily,
"Enter into the ship, and shut thy door." That time came:
The Lord of Storm at even tide caused the heavens to rain
    heavily.
I dreaded the appearance of day;
I was afraid of beholding day:
I entered the ship and shut me my door. . . .

When the seventh day came, storm (and) flood ceased the
    battle . . .
The sea lulled, the blast fell, the flood ceased.
I looked for the people, with a cry of lamentation;
But all mankind had turned again to clay:
The tilled land was become like the waste.
I opened the window, and daylight fell upon my cheeks. . . .

The mountain of the country of Nizir caught the ship . . .
But when the seventh day was come,
I brought out a dove (and) let it go.
The dove went to and fro, but found no foothold, and
    returned.
Then I brought out a swallow (and) let it go.
The swallow went to and fro, but found no foothold, and
    returned.

Then I brought out a raven (and) let it go: The raven went off, noticed the drying of the water, and feeding, wading, croaking, returned not.

Then I brought out (everything) to the four winds, offered victims (sacrifices)

Made an offering of incense on the mountain top. . . .

Nuh-napishtim shall dwell far away, at the mouth of the rivers

Then they took me, and made me dwell far away, at the mouth of the rivers

(the site of Paradise at the mouth of the four rivers including Euphrates).

Conclusion

When we examine the available evidence we can conclude that the mystery of Noah's flood and the survival of humanity and the animal kingdom is a factual account. Although it is a mystery, it is not impossible; nor is it a myth. In fact, our analysis reveals that most of the objections raised by skeptics can be answered quite readily when we consider the remarkable details found in the account in the book of Genesis.

Notes

1. Henry M. Morse, *The Biblical Basis For Modern Science* (Grand Rapids: Baker Book House: 1988) 292.
2. James George Frazer, *Folk-lore in the Old Testament* (London: Macmillan and Co., 1919).
3. C. J. Ball, *Light from the East* (London: Eyre and Spottiswoode, 1899) 34–41.

6

Israel's Exodus from Egypt

The scriptural account of the centuries of bondage of the Jewish captives and their miraculous escape from the armies of Pharaoh during the Exodus has fascinated millions of readers for thousands of years. Consequently, the Exodus takes its place as one of the greatest mysteries found in the pages of Holy Scripture.

There is no other historical account within the Bible, nor in the history of any other people, that contains more miracles and supernatural events than the Bible's account of the liberation of the Jewish people from centuries of bitter slavery in Egypt. Therefore, it is not really surprising that many critics in our secular age have dismissed the biblical account of the Exodus as pure myth, devoid of any historical basis.

The question facing any serious reader of the Bible is this: Can I really believe that the Bible's account of these miraculous events is credible? The critics say no. They claim that there is no independent historical evidence outside the Word of God that supports the captivity of the Jewish people in ancient Egypt.

Furthermore, the critics often state that the Bible stands alone in its claims regarding the remarkable deliverance of the Jews from abject slavery through a series of supernatural plagues and miracles that finally forced the Egyptian pharaoh to release the millions of Jewish slaves that formed the basis of the economy of that ancient land. We will examine fascinating manuscripts from the ancient world as well as recent archeological findings that provide compelling evidence that the Bible's account of the Exodus is historically true.

The biblical account of the Exodus is absolutely fundamental to the history and identity of the Jewish people. In fact, if the Exodus did not actually occur, it would be almost impossible to imagine how such an extraordinary story could have been invented and then incorporated into the three annual public festivals of Passover, Pentecost, and Tabernacles that were observed every year by the whole Jewish people. How could a leader have created the tremendous Exodus story out of thin air and then somehow imposed it upon his people as a true historical event that is now annually observed every Passover "in their generations" forever? It defies common sense.

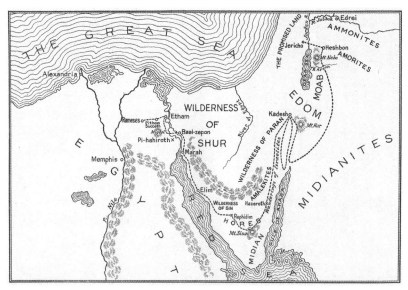

The Journey of Israel.

54

If the Egyptian captivity and Exodus were actually created as a fiction, why would the Jewish people universally accept such an invention as a true historical event? Furthermore, why would the Israelites commemorate this fictional event forever after as the foundational event of the creation of their nation? It is unbelievable that such a fictional event could ever be foisted upon the Jewish people. The Jews have annually celebrated these three great festivals in commemoration of their Exodus for three and a half thousand years. Therefore, logically, the public observance of the Exodus Passover festival can only be explained if the Jewish people actually participated in these remarkable historical events as recorded in the Torah, the first five books of the Bible.

The Bible Writers as Historians

As historical contemporaries of the times, personalities, and the events they recorded, the writers of the Bible were extremely careful and accurate in their recording of historical facts. The historical and archeological discoveries during the last century reveal forty-one names of kings of Israel and surrounding nations that are confirmed by contemporary archeological inscriptions and non-biblical documents. The whole collection of ancient literature fails to reveal a single report from secular historians that can be confirmed through archeology with the same degree of confidence that we can confirm thousands of biblical statements, as well as the details concerning hundreds of personalities and events.

The Jewish people are known for their intelligence and willingness to debate at great length issues involving their religion and history. Is it credible to think that the Jews would universally adopt the complicated religious regulations concerning the three great festivals of Passover, Pentecost, and the Feast of Tabernacles unless their forefathers had begun celebrating these feasts to commemorate the miraculous events of the Exodus? Obviously, such national festivals were transmitted from generation to generation, year by year, father to son, through the centuries. How could this have happened if the original miraculous deliverance from Egypt had never occurred?

Moses, the great lawgiver of Israel, publicly reminded the Jews that they had personally witnessed with their own eyes these miracles and supernatural acts by God to deliver them from the bondage of Egypt:

> And know ye this day: for I speak not with your children which have not known, and which have not seen the chastisement of the Lord your God, his greatness, his mighty hand, and his stretched out arm, and his miracles, and his acts, which he did in the midst of Egypt unto Pharaoh the king of Egypt, and unto all his land; And what he did unto the army of Egypt, unto their horses, and to their chariots; how he made the water of the Red sea to overflow them as they pursued after you, and how the Lord hath destroyed them unto this day; And what he did unto you in the wilderness, until ye came into this place. . . . But your eyes have seen all the great acts of the Lord which he did." (Deuteronomy 11:2–5, 7)

If some unknown creative editor had written the five books of the Torah a thousand years later and tried to get the Jewish

Miracle of the Red Sea. Painting by Wilhelm Ebbinghaus.

people, scattered in diverse communities from Iran to Spain, to universally adopt these festivals in celebration of the Exodus when no one had ever celebrated them before, he would have been denounced as a heretic. At the very least, Jewish rabbis and sages would have conducted strong debates opposing the introduction of such a historical account that no one had seen before. However, there is no record whatsoever that any such debates or discussions ever occurred. The critics' theory of an unknown editor creating the Torah is therefore logically and historically impossible.

Ancient Secular Historians Confirm the Exodus

The Book of Exodus, recounting the supernatural deliverance of the Jews from their bondage in Egypt, is certainly one of the most mysterious, miraculous, and fascinating accounts found in the Bible. Very few Christian pastors or laymen today are aware that we have numerous historical records and ancient inscriptions that provide compelling evidence and confirmation for these key events connected with the creation of the Jewish people as a distinct nation.

The Greek Historian Herodotus

The ancient Greek historian Herodotus wrote about the Exodus in his book *Polymnia:* "This people [the Israelites], by their own account, inhabited the coasts of the Red Sea, but migrated thence to the maritime parts of Syria, all which district, as far as Egypt, is denominated Palestine."[1] The "coasts of the Red Sea" are found in modern-day Egypt, while "the maritime parts of Syria" were partially located on the coastal plain of modern Israel.

The Greek Historian Strabo

It is fascinating to note that Strabo, another Greek historian and geographer, born in 54 B.C., also confirmed the history of the Jews and their escape from Egypt under the leadership of Moses. Strabo wrote in his book *Geography* about Moses: "Among many things believed respecting the temple and inhabitants of Jerusalem, the report most credited is that the Egyptians were the ancestors of the present Jews. An Egyptian priest named Moses, who possessed a portion of the country called lower Egypt, being dissatisfied with the institutions there, left it and came to Judea with a large body of people who worshipped the Divinity."[2]

The Greek Historian Diodorus Siculus

Diodorus Siculus was a Greek historian born in Sicily, who lived from 80–15 B.C. He wrote extensively, creating a set of forty volumes now called the *Library of History*. Diodorus traveled extensively throughout the Middle East, acquiring a vast knowledge of ancient events. In his history, Diodorus reported:

> In ancient times there happened a great plague in Egypt, and many ascribed the cause of it to God, who was offended with them because there were many strangers in the land, by whom foreign rites and ceremonies were employed in their worship of the deity. The Egyptians concluded; therefore, that unless all strangers were driven out of the country, they should never be freed from their miseries. Upon this, as some writers tell us, the most eminent and enterprising of those foreigners who were in Egypt, and obliged to leave the country . . . who retired into the province now called Judea, which was not far from Egypt, and in those times uninhabited. These emigrants were led by Moses, who was superior to all in wisdom and prowess. He gave them laws, and ordained that they should have no images of the gods, because there was only one deity, the heaven, which surrounds all things, and is Lord of the whole.[3]

The Jewish Historian Flavius Josephus

The Jewish historian Flavius Josephus reported that two ancient Egyptian priest-scholars, Manetho and Cheremon, specifically named both Joseph and Moses as leaders of the Jews in their history of Egypt.[4] Josephus recorded that the Egyptians remembered a tradition of an Exodus from their country by the Jews whom they hated because they believed the Israelites were unclean. Manetho and Cheremon stated that the Jews rejected Egyptian customs, including the national worship of Egyptian gods. Most important, these pagan historians acknowledged that the Jews killed the animals that the Egyptians believed were sacred, a reference to the Israelites' practice of sacrificing lambs on that first Passover before they fled from Egypt. These historians also confirmed that the Israelites immigrated into the area of "southern Syria," which was the Egyptian term describing ancient Israel. Perhaps the most important confirmation is found in the statement by Manetho that the sudden Exodus from Egypt occurred in the reign of "Amenophis, son of Rameses, and father of Sethos, who reigned toward the close of the 18th dynasty," which places the Exodus between 1500 and 1400 B.C. This evidence confirms the chronological data found in the Old Testament that suggests the Exodus occurred approximately 1491 B.C.[5]

The Egyptian Ipuwer Papyrus Manuscript

An important Egyptian historical manuscript was discovered in Egypt more than a century ago. Remarkably, this ancient papyrus parallels the history of the Exodus account as found in the Scriptures. This manuscript recorded the writings of an ancient Egyptian named Ipuwer. The papyrus manuscript, now called the Ipuwer Papyrus, was discovered by someone named Anastasi in the area of Memphis, near the pyramids of Saqqara in Egypt. The Museum of Leiden in the Netherlands acquired the papyrus in 1828. The Ipuwer Papyrus was translated and published in English for the first time in 1909 by Professor Alan H. Gardiner, titled *The Admonitions of an Egyptian Sage from a Hieratic Papyrus in Leiden*.[6] Gardiner wrote that the manuscript was one that recorded a genuine historical catastrophe when the whole country of Egypt was in distress and violence. "It is no merely local disturbance that is here described, but a great and overwhelming national disaster." Gardiner suggests that Ipuwer was an Egyptian sage who directed his writing to the king as a complaint that the national catastrophe was in part caused by the king's failure to act and deal with the crisis.

A comparison of several key passages from the biblical book of Exodus with the ancient Egyptian papyrus reveals remarkable correspondences and parallels that point to a real historical catastrophe.

Parallels between the Egyptian Ipuwer Papyrus and the Exodus

Ipuwer Papyrus	*Exodus*
The Plague of Blood	
2:5–6: Plague is throughout the land. Blood is everywhere.	7:21: There was blood throughout all the land of Egypt.
2:10: The river is blood.	7:20: All the waters that were in the river were turned to blood.
2:10: Men shrink from tasting . . . and thirst after water.	7:24: And all the Egyptians digged round about the river for water to drink; for they could not drink of the water of the river.
The Plague of Hail	
9:23: The fire ran along the ground. There was hail, and fire mingled with the hail.	9:25: And the hail smote every herb of the field, and brake every tree of the field.
4:14: Trees are destroyed.	
6:1: No fruit or herbs are found.	
The Plague of Darkness	
9:11: The land is not light.	10:22: And there was a thick darkness in all the land of Egypt.
The Plague of the Egyptian Cattle	
5:5: All animals, their hearts weep. Cattle moan.	9:3: Behold, the hand of the Lord is upon thy cattle which is in the field, upon the horses, upon the asses, upon the camels, upon the oxen, and upon the sheep: there shall be a very grievous murrain [disease].

The Plague of the Firstborn of Egypt	
2:13: He who places his brother in the ground is everywhere.	12:27: He [the Angel of the Lord] smote the Egyptians.
4:3: Forsooth, the children of princes are dashed against the walls.	12:29: At midnight the Lord smote all the firstborn in the land of Egypt.
6:12: Forsooth, the children of princes are cast out in the streets.	12:30: There was not a house where there was not one dead.

Response of the Egyptians to the Loss of their Firstborn	
3:14: It is groaning that is throughout the land, mingled with lamentations.	12:30: There was a great cry in Egypt.

Conclusion

In light of the ample evidence accumulated from ancient Jewish and Greek historians, together with this astonishing Ipuwer Papyrus that parallels several of the ten biblical plagues, it is clear that there is compelling non-biblical evidence to confirm the mysterious scriptural account about the Exodus of the Jews from Egypt.

Notes

1. Herodotus, *Polymnia*, trans. C. 89.
2. Strabo, *Geography*, trans. xvi:c. 2.
3. Diodorus Siculus, *Library of History*, trans. lib. 1., ap Phot.
4. Flavius Josephus, *Josephus Against Apion*, trans. I: 26, 27, 32.
5. Flavius Josephus, *Josephus Against Apion*, trans. I: 26, 27, 32.
6. Alan H. Gardiner, trans. *The Admonitions of an Egyptian Sage from a Hieratic Papyrus in Leiden*, 1909.

7

Was Jesus the Prophet "Like unto Moses"?

There is a strange mystery involving the astonishing similarities between the lives of Moses, Israel's greatest prophet and lawgiver, and Jesus of Nazareth. Fifteen centuries before the birth of Jesus Christ, God prophesied to the Children of Israel that He would raise up a unique prophet, the Messiah, and that they would recognize him by the fact that he would be "a prophet like Moses." Moses himself recorded God's message: "I will raise them up a Prophet from among their brethren, *like unto thee*, and will put my words in his mouth; and he shall speak unto them all that I shall command him" (Deuteronomy 18:18). When the Jewish people went into the Judean desert to hear the extraordinary revival message of John the Baptist, they naturally wanted to know if he was the promised Messiah who was to be a "prophet like Moses." Consequently they asked John, "Art thou *that prophet*?" (John 1:21).

When the disciple Philip recruited Nathanael to join the followers of Jesus, he declared, "We have found him, of whom

Moses in the law, and the prophets, did write, Jesus of Nazareth, the son of Joseph." (John 1:45). After Jesus supernaturally fed five thousand people with a few pieces of bread and fishes, the observers of this miracle naturally referred to this well-known prophecy of Moses, "This is of a truth *that prophet* that should come into the world" (John 6:14). In his defense speech before his death, the martyr Stephen declared that Jesus was the promised Messiah: "This is that Moses, which said unto the children of Israel, A prophet shall the Lord your God raise up unto you of your brethren, like unto me; him shall ye hear. This is he, that was in the church in the wilderness with the angel which spake to him in the mount Sina, and with our fathers: who received the lively oracles to give unto us" (Acts 7:37–38).

Was Jesus' unusual life a remarkable parallel to the career of Moses? Was Jesus "a prophet like Moses"? Absolutely! No other person in history ever came close to fulfilling this particular prophecy except for Jesus of Nazareth. The last verses of Deuteronomy record that even Joshua, Israel's great warrior leader, missed the mark: "And there arose not a prophet since in Israel like unto Moses, whom the Lord knew face to face" (Deuteronomy 34:10).

Moses Teaches the Law. Illustration by Julius Schnorr.

In a complete analysis of the lives of Moses and Jesus of Nazareth, it is astonishing to discover at least fifty similarities in their lives and careers. Many of these factors and events were beyond the control of any normal human. Consider the varied roles that Moses and Jesus both played: prophet, priest, lawgiver, teacher, and leader of men. Both taught people new revelations from God and confirmed the authenticity of their teaching with powerful miracles. Both men spent their early years in Egypt, where they were protected from wicked enemies who sought their death. Moses' family initially rejected his divinely appointed leadership role, but his brother, Aaron, and sister, Miriam, eventually supported him. Jesus' brothers and sisters initially failed to recognize Jesus' leadership role, but his brothers James and Jude later became key leaders in the Church in Jerusalem.

Each leader was considered the wisest man of his generation. Each confronted evil demonic powers and supernaturally subdued them. As Moses appointed seventy rulers over the Children of Israel, Jesus anointed seventy disciples to teach the nations. Moses sent twelve spies to explore Canaan; Jesus sent twelve apostles to reach the world. The Bible does not indicate that either one ever experienced sickness. Neither of their bodies remained buried in a tomb. Moses and Jesus fasted for forty days and both faced supreme spiritual crises on mountaintops. As Moses stretched his hand over the Red Sea to miraculously command the waters to part, Jesus rebuked the dangerous waters of the Sea of Galilee and quieted the waves. Both of their faces shone with the reflected glory of heaven—Moses on Mount Sinai and Jesus on the Mount of Transfiguration.

As Moses rescued Israel from the dead religion of pagan Egypt, Jesus rescued Israel from the dead letter of the Pharisee's law of tradition. Moses and Christ both supernaturally cured lepers and established their spiritual authority through the powerful miracles they performed before numerous witnesses. As Moses conquered the wicked Amalekites — Israel's great enemy — with his arms upraised and a man on either side, Jesus conquered humanity's greatest enemies, sin and death, on the Cross with His arms upraised with a man on either side of Him. Moses lifted up the bronze serpent on a pole in the wilderness to provide healing for his rebellious people; Jesus was lifted up on the Cross to provide healing for the sins to all believers who would repent and turn from their sinful rebellion.

The people were ungrateful and rebelled against the spiritual leadership of both men. The unbelieving people living in those two generations who rebelled against their great leaders ultimately died because of their lack of faith: the first Exodus generation died in the Sinai wilderness, while the second generation died in the brutal Roman siege of Jerusalem in A.D. 70. Moses and Jesus both died on a hill. Moses promised that God would send Israel another Prophet, the Messiah, to lead His people; Jesus promised His followers that His Father would send them another "Comforter," the Holy Spirit to empower His Church.

On the Feast of Passover, both Moses and Jesus offered freedom to all those who placed their faith and trust in God. Several days later, on the Feast of Firstfruits, Moses brought about the resurrection of the Children of Israel as the Jewish slaves miraculously passed through the waters of the Red Sea to escape the centuries of Egyptian bondage; on the anniversary of that same Feast of Firstfruits, Jesus Christ became "the Firstfruits" of resurrection for all Christians when He defeated death, sin, and the grave. Fifty days later, on the Feast of Pentecost, God gave the great gift of the Torah, the Law of God, to Israel and the nations. Fifty days after His own resurrection, Jesus Christ gave the Church the great gift of the baptism of the Holy Spirit.

The evidence is compelling that Jesus Christ was "that prophet" like unto Moses that the righteous Jewish believers of Israel had longed for during fourteen centuries since the time of the Exodus. Therefore, Jesus of Nazareth is truly the promised Messiah.

8

The Ashes of the Red Heifer

One of the most unusual mysteries involving the worship practices of the Jews in ancient Israel concerned the ashes from the sacrifice of the red heifer. Many passages in the *Talmud*, the Jewish commentary on the Bible, explore the meaning of this very strange sacrifice. The Bible describes the red heifer sacrifice as follows:

> This is the ordinance of the law which the Lord hath commanded, saying, Speak unto the children of Israel, that they bring thee a red heifer without spot, wherein is no blemish, and upon which never came yoke. . . . And one shall burn the heifer in his sight; her skin, and her flesh, and her blood, with her dung, shall he burn. . . . And a man that is clean shall gather up the ashes of the heifer, and lay them up without the camp in a clean place, and it shall be kept for the congregation of the children of Israel for a water of separation: it is a purification for sin." (Numbers 19:2, 5, 9)

During the forty years that the Israelites wandered in the wilderness, God instructed the Jews that the blood of the red heifer sacrifice was to be sprinkled opposite the entrance to the Tabernacle. When the Temple was finally built in Jerusalem four centuries later, this unusual sacrifice of the red heifer took place on a small plateau on the western slope of the Mount of Olives, directly opposite the Eastern Gate and the Holy of Holies of Solomon's Temple.

During a research trip to Israel, I followed the precise eyewitness description by the greatest medieval Jewish rabbi, Moses Maimonides, as detailed in his famous commentary on the Law known as the *Mishneh Torah, Hilchos Bais Habechirah* (The Law of God's Chosen House). Writing about the very low wall above the Eastern Gate, Maimonides declared, "Thus the priest [who offered the Para Aduma—the Red Heifer] could see the opening of the Temple when he sprinkled its blood, while standing on the Mount of Olives."[1]

There I found the exact spot on the Mount of Olives described as the place for the red heifer sacrifice. According to the *Mishneh Torah*, the ceremonial burning of the red heifer occurred only seven times in Jewish history: once by Moses, once by Ezra, and five other times until the destruction of the Second Temple by the Roman armies in 70 A.D. Every time, the final few ashes that remained from the previous sacrifices were carefully added to the new ashes to provide a sacred continuity—a perpetual sacrifice.

After being slaughtered by the young priest with a large knife, the body of the red heifer was completely burned with cedar wood, hyssop, and scarlet within a large bonfire on the plateau opposite the Temple and city. Then the priest would gather the ashes in a clay vessel and return to the Temple. Because this unusual sacrifice defiled one until sunset, the priest who performed this ceremony could not be the high priest or the high priest's son. Some of the ashes were sprinkled on the surface of water in one of the huge subterranean cisterns beneath the surface of the Temple Mount. The ashes and water produced the "waters of purification" needed to purify people who had become ritually defiled by touching a dead body in a funeral. The Jews believed that the inevitable presence of dead men's bones in the ground surrounding an ancient city inevitably spiritually defiled a holy place.

The aim of this particular sacrifice was to purify someone from the defilement of death, yet the young priest who obediently completed the sacrifice of the red heifer became defiled (unclean) himself until the evening of the day of sacrifice. One commentary states that this sacrifice "purifies the impure, and at the same time renders impure the pure! So inscrutable was its nature that they said that even King Solomon in all his wisdom despaired of ever learning the secret meaning of divine laws regarding the red heifer sacrifice."[2] Despite the fact that the "waters of purification" produced from the ashes from the red heifer sacrifice were absolutely essential for the cleansing of any Jew about to enter the Temple, even the celebrated wisdom of King Solomon failed to fully understand the nature of the red heifer sacrifice. When King Solomon wrote, "I said, I will be wise, but it was far from me" (Ecclesiastes 7:23), the Jewish commentary known as the *Mishneh* claimed that he alluded to his inability to comprehend the profound paradoxes connected with God's law concerning the sacrifice of the ashes of the red heifer. Apparently, the fact that the priest who obediently fulfilled God's instructions concerning this red heifer sacrifice was himself became "unclean" until evening was beyond the ability of Solomon to understand.

The book of Hebrews suggests that the sacrifice of the ashes of the red heifer and the resulting "waters of purification" are a symbol of the ultimate sacrifice of Jesus Christ for our sins. In an analogous fashion, Christ "became sin for us" during His sacrifice on the Cross in order that we might become the righteousness of Christ. The red heifer was a pure sacrifice, without blemish, and was the only animal sacrificed outside the walls of the city. In an obvious parallel, Jesus became the pure sacrifice for us, without blemish, sacrificed outside the walls of Jerusalem. Curiously, the red heifer sacrifice was one of the very few authorized sacrifices for which God demanded a female animal. Almost all other sacrifices were of male animals.

It is fascinating to note that Jesus was betrayed by Judas for precisely thirty pieces of silver, the exact price of a female slave. A "pure" red heifer is very rare. Almost all cattle have some imperfections in their coloring. The *Talmud* states that even one white hair would disqualify the heifer for the red heifer sacrifice. Not only did the heifer have to be 100 percent red, it could not have had a yoke laid upon its neck. *Time* magazine reported on October 16, 1989, that the chief rabbi of Israel sent a team of scientists to Europe in August to obtain frozen embryos from a breed of red heifers that will be used to raise a pure red heifer on an Israeli cattle ranch.[3] The extraordinary part of this report is that this proves the highest Jewish authorities, the two chief rabbis, have decided to make practical preparations to enable Israel to begin to conduct animal sacrifices once again after almost two thousand years. Several years ago the Jewish religious authorities believed they had found a pure red heifer and raised the animal on a farm owned by orthodox Jews near Mount Carmel, in northern Israel. However, after several years the religious authorities noted that several white hairs had appeared on the animal, disqualifying it as a pure red heifer. In 2002, the Temple Institute authorities (who have carefully constructed many of the objects to be used in a future Temple according to the Torah and *Mishneh*) announced that another red heifer has been located similar to the one being raised in Israel near Mount Carmel.

Two millennia after their beloved Temple was burned to the ground in A.D. 70, some Jews in Israel are preparing to resume the Temple sacrifice system. According to the Talmud and the rabbis, it is essential that Israel resume this sacrifice in order to cleanse the Temple Mount and priesthood. Obviously, the entire Temple Mount has been repeatedly defiled by both ritual impurity and the deaths of hundreds of thousands of soldiers, priests, and others during the intervening years since A.D. 70. These years of desecration and death have made the Temple Mount ceremonially impure for worship as commanded by the Old Testament laws of God. It will be necessary to cleanse the Temple area, the rocks, the Temple vessels, and the priests as well, using the waters of purification on which ashes of the red heifer will be sprinkled. Then a new Sanhedrin, a religious court composed of senior rabbis, can resume the ancient Temple sacrifice system as described by the prophet Daniel. "And from the time that the daily sacrifice shall be taken away, and the abomination that maketh desolate set up, there shall be a thousand two hundred and ninety days." (Daniel 12:11). The prophet Ezekiel foretold that the sacred vessels and linen robes would be prepared for use in the future Temple in the Millennium: "They shall enter into my sanctuary, and they shall come near to my table, to minister unto me, and they shall keep my charge. And it shall come to pass, that when they enter in at the gates of the inner court, they shall be clothed with linen garments; and no wool shall come upon them, whiles they minister in the gates of the inner court, and within" (Ezekiel 44:16–17).

It is significant that the Temple Institute in the Old City of Jerusalem has already constructed over eighty of the special sacred objects, vessels, and linen priestly garments that the Bible teaches are required for future Temple services. Several Orthodox yeshivas (Jewish Bible seminaries) in Jerusalem have trained five hundred male Jewish Kohanien students (who are descendants from Aaron and the tribe of Levi) to fulfill duties of Temple worship and sacrifice. Many have been trained in the Temple worship rituals and have learned to play the restored biblical musical instruments, such as the ancient lyre as used by King David.

The prophet Ezekiel indicates that Israel will resume the mysterious sacrifice of the ashes of the red heifer in the last days in connection with the resumption of Temple services. "Then will I sprinkle clean water upon you, and ye shall be clean: from all your filthiness, and from all your idols, will I cleanse you" (Ezekiel 36:25). In addition to the obvious spiritual significance of the law of the sacrifice of the red heifer, we now understand that the water of purification described in Numbers 19 actually had the ability to destroy germs and infection. The resulting water of purification solution contained ashes from the red heifer sacrifice combined with cedar, hyssop, and scarlet thread. This water of purification contained "cedar" oil that came from a kind of juniper tree that grew in both Israel and in the Sinai. This cedar oil would irritate the skin, encouraging the person to vigorously rub the solution into their hands. Most important, the hyssop tree (associated with mint, possibly marjoram) would produce hyssop oil. This hyssop oil is actually a very effective antiseptic and antibacterial agent. Hyssop oil contains 50 percent carvacrol, which is a fungicidal and antibacterial agent still used in medicine today, according to Doctor S. I. McMillen's book *None of These Diseases* [4]

When we note that the waters of purification from the red heifer sacrifice were to be used to cleanse someone who had become defiled and unclean due to touching a dead body, we begin to understand that this law was not only spiritual, but for medical purposes. The writer of the book of Hebrews (probably the apostle Paul), as a well-educated Jewish rabbi, understood that the red heifer sacrifice had a practical medical effect in addition to its more obvious spiritual element. The book of Hebrews declared that "the blood of bulls and of goats, and the ashes of an heifer sprinkling the unclean, sanctifieth to the purifying of the flesh" (Hebrews 9:13).

The Jews were unique in comparison to the pagan nations surrounding them in their strict attention to sanitation measures and personal cleanliness in obedience to the commands of God as revealed in the Old Testament. [5] As a result of the strict medical laws given by God, the Jewish people were blessed with much better health, as well as a significantly improved mortality rate that was positively impacted by their superior sanitation and biblically sanctioned medical practices.

Notes

1. Moses Maimonides, *Mishneh Torah, Hilchos Bais Habechirah* (Jerusalem: Maznaim Publishing Corp., 1986) Chapter 6, section 6.
2. Talmud Reference.
3. *Time.* 16 Oct. 1989.
4. S. I. McMillen, *None Of These Diseases* (Minneapolis: Successful Living, 1972).
5. Grant R. Jeffrey, *The Signature of God* (Toronto: Frontier Research Publications, Inc., 1996) 139–159.

9

The Destruction of Tyre

One of the most unusual of all the mysteries found in the Word of God is that account of the prophecy and history of the destruction of the ancient city of Tyre. The famous Phoenician city, known as the "Queen of the Sea," was located twenty miles south of the present city of Sidon on the Lebanese coast of the Mediterranean. Tyre was enormously powerful, proud, and rich, receiving the trade and tribute of many lesser cities; it was the equivalent of New York City in its day. Despite the overwhelming power and dominant position of Tyre, the prophet Ezekiel (592–570 B.C.) proclaimed an unusual prophetic vision that outlined an unprecedented series of military invasions that would ultimately result in the destruction of the famous city.

The Vision of Tyre's Destruction by the Prophet Ezekiel

Therefore thus saith the Lord God; Behold, I am against thee, O Tyrus, and will cause many nations to come up against thee, as the sea causeth his waves to come up.

And they shall destroy the walls of Tyrus, and break down her towers: I will also scrape her dust from her, and make her like the top of a rock. It shall be a place for the spreading of nets in the midst of the sea: for I have spoken it, saith the Lord God: and it shall become a spoil to the nations. . . .

For thus saith the Lord God; Behold, I will bring upon Tyrus Nebuchadrezzar king of Babylon, a king of kings, from the north, with horses, and with chariots, and with horsemen, and companies, and much people. He shall slay with the sword thy daughters in the field: and he shall make a fort against thee, and cast a mount against thee, and lift up the buckler against thee. . . .

And they shall make a spoil of thy riches, and make a prey of thy merchandise: and they shall break down thy walls, and destroy thy pleasant houses: and they shall lay thy stones and thy timber and thy dust in the midst of the water. . . .

And I will make thee like the top of a rock: thou shalt be a place to spread nets upon; thou shalt be built no more: for I the Lord have spoken it, saith the Lord God. . . .

I will make thee a terror, and thou shalt be no more: though thou be sought for, yet shalt thou never be found again, saith the Lord God. (Ezekiel 26:3–5, 7–8, 12, 14, 21)

To better understand the predictions of Ezekiel, it may help to outline the specific detailed predictions as follows:

1. God will bring upon Tyre Nebuchadnezzar king of Babylon (26:8).
2. God will "cause many nations to come up against thee" "as waves to come up" (26:3).
3. They will destroy the walls of Tyre, and "make her like the top of a rock" (26:4).
4. It shall be "a place for the spreading of nets" (26:5).
5. Tyre's enemies will lay the destroyed city's debris "in the midst of the waters" (26:12).

6. The original destroyed city of Tyre will be "built no more" (26:14).
7. The ancient city of Tyre will "never be found again" (26: 21).

While Ezekiel's prophecy of Tyre's destruction initially seems contradictory on its surface, the subsequent history reveals the unprecedented way in which these predictions were finally fulfilled. When we compare Ezekiel's prophecies about Tyre with the history of the city, we will be amazed to witness the remarkable fulfillment of the Word of God.

First Prophecy:
King Nebuchadnezzar's Defeat of Mainland Tyre

Only three years after Ezekiel received and published his prophecy about Tyre's destruction, the king of Babylon, Nebuchadnezzar, began his prolonged siege against the powerful mainland city of Tyre. The *Encyclopedia Britannica* reports: "After a 13-year siege (585–573 B.C.) by Nebuchadnezzar II, Tyre made terms and acknowledged Babylonian suzerainty."[1] However, when Nebuchadnezzar's army broke through the gates of Tyre, he was disappointed to discover that the city was virtually deserted. Most of the population had evacuated the mainland city by ship and relocated on a small island only half a mile off the coast. The resourceful citizens of Tyre used their incredible wealth and the help of many strong allies to fortify the new city walls that they rapidly erected on the island. The mainland city of Tyre was destroyed in 573 B.C. by the powerful armies of Babylon under Nebuchadnezzar's military leadership; however, the newly built city of Tyre on the island remained a powerful and well-defended city for several centuries, protected by its fleet, its allies, and its unique defensive position as an island fortress.

Second Prophecy:
A Series of Attacks Like Waves of the Sea

The next prophecy was fulfilled during the invasion of the Middle East by the victorious armies of Alexander the Great (333 B.C.). According to the *Encyclopædia Britannica*, "In his war on the

Persians Alexander III [the Great], after defeating Darius III at the Battle of Issus, marched southward toward Egypt, calling upon the Phoenician cities to open their gates, as it was part of his general plan to deny their use to the Persian fleet. The citizens of Tyre refused to do so, and Alexander laid siege to the city. Possessing no fleet, he demolished old Tyre, on the mainland, and with the debris built a mole [causeway] 200 ft. (60 meters) wide across the straits separating the old and new towns, erecting towers and war engines at the farther end."[1] Alexander built up his own fleet of ships from the contributions of his allies and eventually completed the causeway to destroy the island city of Tyre, capturing and then selling thirty thousand citizens into slavery as well as killing over eight thousand defenders.

The ancient Roman historian Curtius wrote about the construction of Alexander's causeway by the Greek army. He wrote that Alexander the Great used material that was available from both Mount Libanus and the old city of Tyre to supply stones and dirt for the causeway.[2]

Just as ocean waves come in a series or succession, the armies of Tyre's surrounding enemies came one after another over the centuries in a continued series of invasions to destroy the greatest city of the ancient Mediterranean coast.

Third Prophecy:
Tyre's Walls Would Be Destroyed

The historian Philip Myers wrote about the Greek army's total destruction of the island city of Tyre. "Alexander the Great . . . reduced it to ruins (332 B.C.). She recovered in a measure from this blow, but never regained the place she had previously held in the world. The larger part of the site of the once great city is now bare as the top of a rock."[3]

Fourth prophecy:
Tyre Would Be "A Place for the Spreading of Nets"

Despite the ideal location of the city based on its harbor and its tremendous fresh water supply, the mainland city was left bare as a rock, exactly as the prophecy of the Bible had predicted centuries earlier. The historian Philip Myers wrote, "The larger part of the site of the once great city is now bare as the top of a rock, where the fisherman that still frequent the spot spread their nets to dry."[3] The archeologist Hans-Wolf Rackl described the present situation of the site of ancient Tyre: "Today hardly a single stone of the old Tyre remains intact. . . . Tyre has become a place, to dry fish nets,' as the prophet predicted."[4]

Fifth Prophecy:
Tyre's Debris "In the Midst of the Waters"

As pointed out above, Alexander the Great's army took the debris of stone and timber from the destroyed mainland city of Tyre and cast it into the sea to create a causeway to enable his army to approach the satellite island city with their engines of war to destroy it.

Sixth Prophecy:
Ancient Tyre Was to Be "Built No More"

Many people have assumed that this prophecy was incorrect, in that any map of the Middle East clearly reveals that there is a city called Tyre located on the Mediterranean Coast of the nation of Lebanon today. However, the modern city of Tyre is not the rebuilt city of ancient Tyre. The ancient ruins remain as they were in ancient times, still abandoned to the use of Lebanese fishermen who dry their nets on its bare rocks in fulfillment of the Bible's prophecy. It would be the equivalent of the destruction of New York City and the development of a new city built centuries later many miles to the north, which took the ancient name to honor the memory.

Others have complained that there is a small fishing village built near the ancient ruins of Tyre. However, this is no contradiction. The prophecy that the fishermen will dry their nets on the bare rocks on the ruins of ancient Tyre obviously implies that these fishermen would live nearby. Nina Jidejian wrote, "The 'Sidonian' port of Tyre is still in use today. Small fishing vessels lay at anchor there. An examination of the foundations reveals granite columns of the Roman period which were incorporated as binders in the walls by the Crusaders. The port has become a haven today for fishing boats and a place for spreading nets."[5]

Although almost all destroyed ancient cities were rebuilt in time because of the obvious advantages of their geographical location, trade routes, water sources, roads, etc., the ancient ruins of Tyre remain as silent testimony to the accuracy of the Bible's prophecies. The scientist Peter Stoner wrote of the incredible odds against Tyre never being rebuilt in light of its natural advantages as a site for a city. Stoner wrote, "The great freshwater springs of Reselain are at the site of the mainland city of Tyre, and no doubt supplied the city with an abundance of fresh water. These springs are still there and still flow, but their water runs into the sea. The flow of these springs was measured by an engineer, and found to be about 10,000,000 gallons daily. It is still an excellent site for a city and would have free water enough for a large modern city, yet it has never been rebuilt."[6]

Seventh Prophecy:
The Ancient City "Will Never Be Found"

The prophet Ezekiel's expression that the destroyed city of Tyre "will never be found" obviously does not mean that the physical site of the ruined city could never be located, because the site cannot cease to exist. Ezekiel's expression therefore logically refers to the fact that, although people would desire to see the magnificent city rebuilt, the city of Tyre would never be found as a rebuilt city again.

Floyd E. Hamilton wrote in his book *The Basis of the Christian Faith*: "Other cities destroyed by enemies had been rebuilt; Jerusalem was destroyed many times, but always has risen again from the ruins. . . . The voice of God has spoken and Old Tyre today stands as it has for twenty-five centuries, a bare rock, uninhabited by man! Today anyone who wants to see the site of the old city can have it pointed out to him along the shore, but there is not a ruin to mark the spot. It has been scraped clean and has never been rebuilt."[7]

Some critics have questioned the apparent contradiction between the prophecy in Ezekiel 26:8 regarding the imminent destruction of the city of Tyre by the armies of King Nebuchadnezzar and the statement found a few chapters later in Ezekiel 29:18 that describes the failure of the king to capture the riches of the city of Tyre to enable him to pay his army from the spoils of war. "Son of man, Nebuchadrezzar king of Babylon caused his army to serve a great service against Tyrus: every head was made bald, and every shoulder was peeled: yet had he no wages, nor his army, for Tyrus, for the service that he had served against it" (Ezekiel 29:18). However, there is no contradiction in the mind of the author Ezekiel nor in the actual historical statement. Although the Babylonian army destroyed the mainland city of Tyre, they obviously failed to profit from the spoils, possibly because the burning of the city at the end of the brutal siege prevented successful looting of the enormous wealth of the city.

The City of Tyre Today

Nina Jidejian concludes in her excellent book, *Tyre through the Ages,* that city of Tyre's,

> . . . stones may be found as far away as Acre and Beirut. Yet evidences of a great past are abundant and recent excavations have revealed successive levels of this proud Phoenician seaport. . . . The great ancient city of Tyre lay buried under accumulated debris. The ruins of an aqueduct and a few scattered columns and the ruins of a Christian basilica were the only remains found above ground. . . . Looking down into the water one can see a mass of granite columns and stone blocks strewn over the sea bottom. Until recently the ruins of Tyre above water were few.[5]

The detailed prophecy about the repeated invasions and final defeat of the rich and powerful city of Tyre is clearly one of the most fascinating and improbable predictions made in the Word of God. Yet every single detail of this complicated prophecy made by the prophet Ezekiel twenty-six centuries ago has come true with precision. The history of Tyre, once the greatest city of the ancient world, stands as a silent witness to the authority and supernatural inspiration of the Word of God.

Notes

1. "Tyre," *Encyclopædia Britannica*, 1970 edition.
2. Quintius Curtius, Title of Work. trans. 18–19.
3. Philip Myers, *General History for Colleges and High Schools* (Boston: Ginn and Company, 1889).
4. Hans-Wolf Rackl, *Archaeolology Underwater*, trans. Ronald J. Floyd (New York: Charles Scribner's Sons, 1968) 179.
5. Nina Jidejian, *Tyre Through the Ages* (Beirut: Dar El-Mashreq Publishers, 1969) 139.
6. Peter Stoner, *Science Speaks: An Evaluation of Certain Christian Evidences* (Chicago: Moody Press, 1963) 76–77.
7. Floyd E. Hamilton, *The Basis of the Christian Faith* (New York: George H. Doran Company, 1927) 299.

10

The Lost Ark of the Covenant

Three and a half thousand years ago, God commanded Moses to build an object of great beauty and cover it with precious gold. This was the sacred Ark of the Covenant, the most powerful spiritual object the world had ever seen. God's special Shekinah glory dwelt above the mercy seat upon the Ark of the Covenant. God's Ark of the Covenant guided and supernaturally protected Israel. When the Israelites carried the Ark before them in battle in obedience to God, their enemies were destroyed. The fortress city of Jericho collapsed after the Ark was carried in procession seven times around the city when the Israelites first entered the Holy Land. Centuries later, Israel's pagan enemies the Philistines conquered the Jewish army when the evil leadership of the two sons of the prophet Samuel allowed the Ark to be carried forth without God's direction. However, the Philistines' pagan idols supernaturally fell before the presence of the Shekinah glory of God that dwelt on the mercy seat of the Ark. When the Philistines returned the Ark, the people of the tribe of Benjamin sacrilegiously opened the lid of the Ark to see the sacred tablets of the Law; fifty thousand of them were struck with plague.

The Making of the Ark of the Covenant

During the first year of Israel's wandering in the wilderness, God gave specific directions to Moses to create the Tabernacle and a number of sacred objects, patterned after the worship objects that exist eternally in the Temple in heaven: "According to all that I shew thee, after the pattern of the tabernacle, and the pattern of all the instruments thereof, even so shall ye make it." (Exodus 25:9). The building of these holy objects would provide an expression of His eternal covenant with His chosen people.

The most significant of these objects was the Ark of the Covenant. God gave explicit instructions to Moses regarding his building of the sacred Ark of the Covenant (Exodus 25). The word *ark* is derived from the Hebrew word that identifies a chest, box, or coffin. The Ark was built of strong acacia wood and then covered with gold within and without. The Ark's dimensions were forty-five by twenty-seven by twenty-seven inches. It was covered with a lid of pure gold, called the mercy seat. Two gold cherubim facing each other from the two ends

Model of Ark of the Covenant.

of the lid represented the angelic cherubim who surround the throne of God in heaven. The Lord said that His divine presence would dwell with the Ark forever. This "Shekinah" glory filled the tribes of Israel with awe and reverence.

Israel was instructed to place a number of sacred objects in the Ark of the Covenant. The first of these sacred objects was the rod of Aaron. Aaron, the first high priest, used this rod to perform miracles before the Pharaoh of Egypt. Also included in the Ark was the manna, the daily bread from heaven that God provided for forty years in the Sinai wilderness. Last were the two tablets of stone on which God had written the Ten Commandments. Aaron's rod symbolized God's sovereign choice and the supernatural deliverance of Israel from Egypt. The bowl of manna symbolized God's daily provision for His people. The two stone tablets of the Law represented God's concern for His people, as He gave them His divine law to guide them. All of these sacred objects, especially the Ark of the Covenant, revealed God's presence in the life of Israel and prophetically pointed to our salvation in Jesus Christ.

God gave instructions to Moses regarding the proper handling and care of the Ark by the Levites and priests (see Exodus 25:10–22). The holiness and divine presence of God surrounding the Ark of the Covenant was so overpowering that improper handling resulted in instant death. The Lord commanded that only the Levites were to carry the Ark, and then only by resting the poles that extended from the ends of the Ark on their shoulders. One time King David violated God's instructions and carelessly ordered the priests to carry the Ark in an ox cart instead of using the method God had commanded Moses. The oxen stumbled, and the cart began to tip over. Uzzah reached out to keep the Ark from falling and died because of his violation of the laws of God regarding transportation and handling of the Ark. Perhaps the many years of storing the Ark in Abinadab's house caused his son, Uzzah, to lose his sense of reverence for the holiness of God's presence that surrounded the Ark. On another occasion, after the Ark was recaptured from the Philistines, the Jewish men of Bethshemesh, out of curiosity, violated its sanctity by opening the Ark. This violation of the Ark caused more than fifty thousand people to die of the plague.

The Importance of the Ark of the Covenant

When it was finished, the Ark of the Covenant was placed in the Tabernacle of worship that was then moved from place to place throughout the Sinai wilderness at God's discretion as Israel wandered forty years in the wilderness. Finally, the priests carried the Ark through the miraculously dried-up riverbed of the Jordan River into the Promised Land on the tenth day of the month Nisan: "And the priests that bare the ark of the covenant of the Lord stood firm on dry ground in the midst of Jordan, and all the Israelites passed over on dry ground, until all the people were passed clean over Jordan" (Joshua 3:17).

In the famous battle of Jericho, the priests carried the Ark around the city seven times. The walls miraculously fell, and the Israelites marched over the collapsed walls into the city (Joshua 6). As documented in my book *The Signature of God*,[1] the archeologist Dr. John Garstang discovered in 1930–1936 that the walls of Jericho had actually collapsed just as the book of Joshua records. For centuries afterward, the Israelites victoriously carried the Ark into battle against the pagan armies that opposed them.

When the first Temple was completed under King Solomon, the Ark was placed in the Holy of Holies. The Bible describes this dramatic event: "And the priests brought in the ark of the covenant of the Lord unto his place, into the oracle of the house, to the most holy place, even under the wings of the cherubims" (1 Kings 8:6).

What Happened to the Ark of the Covenant?

The Ark remained in the Temple until the final years of King Solomon's reign when, according to many sources, it was taken to Ethiopia. From the time of Solomon onward, the Bible is strangely silent about the location of the Ark. We know it was not present in the Second Temple when the Jewish captives returned from the Babylonian captivity in 536 B.C. Yet, according to the prophet Jeremiah, the Ark of the Covenant will still play a pivotal role in our future. He prophesied in Jeremiah 3:15–17 that, just before the return of the Messiah, the people of Israel would once again visit and be concerned with the Ark of the Covenant. However, when the Messiah returns to set up His kingdom, the Bible prophesies that the Ark will cease to be the central focus of Israel's worship. Then, they will worship Jesus Christ as their Messiah directly. This prophecy implies that the Ark will play a crucial role in the prophetic events leading up to the rebuilding of the Temple and the return of the Messiah.

Several biblical commentators, including Dr. David Lewis and Arthur Bloomfield, have written about scriptural predictions that the lost Ark will return to the Temple Mount in the last days.[2,3] The prophecies of the Bible suggest that, after being hidden for almost three thousand years, the Ark will once again take its place at the forefront of human history. If the Ark of the Covenant still exists and is publicly presented, I believe that the Jewish religious and political leadership of Israel would be compelled to rebuild the Temple with the Holy of Holies to provide a sacred repository for this extraordinary object. The Scripture's prophecies reveal that the religious leaders of Israel will also resume the ancient animal sacrifices in fulfillment of Daniel's prophecy (Daniel 12:11).

In his detailed prophecy describing the coming Russian-Arab invasion of Israel (the War of Gog and Magog), the prophet Ezekiel recorded God's declaration: "And I will set my glory among the heathen, and all the heathen shall see my judgment that I have executed, and my hand that I have laid upon them. So the house of Israel shall know that I am the Lord their God from that day and forward" (Ezekiel 39:21–22). The words "my glory" may refer to the Shekinah glory of God dwelling above the mercy seat of the Ark. Throughout the Scriptures the phrase "my glory" is used exclusively in reference to either the Shekinah glory surrounding the Ark of the Covenant or to Jesus Christ, Israel's Messiah. The context of Ezekiel 39:21 strongly suggests that the Ark is in view in Ezekiel's prophecy because there is no mention in this particular prophecy of the return of the Messiah to set up His Kingdom.

To discover the truth about the Ark of the Covenant, we will need to examine evidence from two different sources: (1)

the secular history of ancient Ethiopia and (2) the prophecies and historical records of the Bible. These records will enable us to determine the probable location of the Ark and its possible prophetic role in the future.

The last time the Ark of the Covenant was unquestionably in the hands of Israel is reported in 2 Chronicles 8:11, in which Solomon asked his wife, the pagan daughter of the Egyptian pharaoh, to leave the area where the sacred Ark of the Covenant was stored because she was not a true believer in Jehovah. Shortly after this event, the Ark of the Covenant, the most important and powerful spiritual object in Israel's history, disappeared from the national life of the Jewish state. In all of the Bible's subsequent accounts of battles, rebellions, invasions, and the looting of the Temple by various pagan empires, the Scriptures are strangely silent about the location of this most sacred and powerful Ark of the Covenant.

There is one brief mention of an "ark" in 2 Chronicles 35: 3, where King Josiah orders the priests to return the ark to the Temple. It had been removed earlier by a wicked king to make room for his pagan idols. However, it is unlikely that this "ark"

The Ark Returns. Painting by Gustave Doré.

object referred to in 2 Chronicles 35:3 is the true Ark of the Covenant because the biblical writer does not use its proper name, "the Ark of the Covenant." Also, in light of the terrible divine punishment given to past defilers of the true Ark, such as Uzzah and those fifty thousand struck with plague from Beth-shemesh, it is difficult to believe that an evil king could have simply removed the true Ark of the Covenant and substituted false idols in the Temple without suffering divine retribution. However, if the Ethiopian historical records are correct, then the "ark" object referred to in 2 Chronicles 35:3 was only a replica of the true Ark of the Covenant. This would explain how they could have removed this "ark" with impunity.

The Ethiopian Royal Chronicles

During the reign of King Solomon, the famous Queen of Sheba visited Solomon in Jerusalem several years after he placed the Ark of the Covenant in the Holy of Holies of his newly built Temple. Second Chronicles 9:12 hints at the king providing the Queen of Sheba with a son when it tells us, "And King Solomon gave to the Queen of Sheba *all her desire, whatsoever she asked*, beside that which she had brought unto the king. So she turned, and went away to her own land, she and her servants." We know from the Bible that Solomon was not opposed to marrying foreign women and siring children. According to the Ethiopian history, the Queen of Sheba married King Solomon and they had a son to continue the royal line. The Ethiopian royal chronicles record that Prince Menelik I of Ethiopia was the son of King Solomon and the Queen of Sheba. He lived in the palace in Jerusalem with his father, King Solomon, until his maturity. While being educated by the priests of the Temple, he became a strong believer in Jehovah.

In a September 1935 article in *National Geographic*,[4] Leo Roberts recorded his interviews with various priests in different parts of Ethiopia, all of whom consistently told the following story:

> The Queen of Sheba had visited King Solomon and had a child, Menelik I. Solomon educated the lad in Jerusalem until he was nineteen years old. The boy then returned to Ethiopia with a large group of Jews, taking with him

the true Ark of the Covenant. Many people believe that this Ark is now in some church along the northern boundary of present-day Ethiopia, near Aduwa (Adua) or Aksum. But if it is here, it is so well guarded by the priests that no student from the Western world has been able to confirm or deny the legend.

An *Encyclopedia Britannica* article also confirms this tradition.[5] "It [Aksum-Aduwa] contains the ancient church where, according to tradition, the Tabot, or Ark of the Covenant, brought from Jerusalem by the son of Solomon and the Queen of Sheba, was deposited and is still supposed to rest."

Menelik I, as a royal son of Solomon, was the founder of the longest-lived monarchy in history. His royal dynasty extended from King Solomon to the late Emperor Haile Selassie (he called himself the "Lion of Judah") to the present emperor, all of whom claim direct descent from King Solomon. During the 1974 communist military coup in Ethiopia, Emperor Haile Selassie was imprisoned and then assassinated in jail the following year under mysterious circumstances. The Marxist Ethiopian government secretly buried him in an unmarked grave. However, a number of Haile Selassie's royal descendants escaped and are now living in the West. The current emperor is living in England.

Prince Stephen Mengesha, the great-grandson of Emperor Haile Selassie, who lives in Canada, was kind enough to be interviewed. He confirmed my research about the importance of the Ark of the Covenant in Ethiopian history. Prince Mengesha's father, Prince Mengesha Sevoum, was governor-general of Ethiopia, overseeing the northern province of Tigre and the ancient city of Aksum, where the Ark was secretly hidden in a subterranean repository and was guarded by the custodians of the religious relics thousands of years ago. Prince Mengesha Sevoum was the director of an Ethiopian relief operation in the Sudan. He appeared in an interview on *Praise the Lord*, a national television program in the United States in the fall of 1988 and verified that the Ark of the Covenant was still being protected in Ethiopia at that time. He showed official government photos of Queen Elizabeth II, Prince Philip, and Emperor Haile Selassie during their royal visit to Aksum, when the Queen and Prince privately visited the repository of the ancient Ark of the Covenant.

Prince Stephen Mengesha spent several summers as a teenager exploring the region of Aksum (located in northern Ethiopia) and visited many of the ancient and almost inaccessible stone churches where early Ethiopian Jewish Christians held their services. He confirmed that the subterranean chambers of the historic Church of Zion of Mary in Aksum held the ancient repository of the Ark of the Covenant.

The Ethiopian official royal historical records, known as the *Glory of the Kings* (*Kebra-Nagast*), report on what happened to the Ark of the Covenant. There are several detailed Ethiopian murals that depict how Prince Menelik I took the Ark to Ethiopia for safekeeping three thousand years ago. When the Queen of Sheba died, nineteen-year-old Prince Menelik I prepared to leave Jerusalem to return twenty-five hundred miles to his native country to become king. Before he departed, King Solomon (to whom the prince bore an uncanny resemblance in beauty and regal bearing) ordered his craftsmen to create a perfect replica of the Ark for his son to take with him to Ethiopia. The great distance between the two royal cities would prevent the prince from worshiping at the Temple in Jerusalem.

However, the Ethiopian records suggest that Prince Menelik was very concerned with the growing spiritual apostasy in Israel's religious and political leadership. His father, Solomon, was now allowing idols to be placed in the sacred Temple to please his pagan wives. Solomon gave the prince a going-away banquet. After the officials were filled with wine, Menelik and his loyal associates among the Jewish priesthood allegedly switched the replica ark with the true Ark. He then took the true Ark of the Covenant home to Ethiopia to Aksum, the ancient capital of the Queen of Sheba. The Ethiopian royal chronicles claim he left the perfect replica of the ark in the Holy of Holies in Jerusalem.

The Ethiopian royal archives record that a group of Jewish priests, along with representatives from each of Israel's twelve tribes, reverently took the true Ark to Ethiopia for safekeeping until Israel's leaders repented of their sin of pagan idol worship and returned to the pure worship of God. Unfortunately, throughout the last three thousand years, Israel never truly repented as a nation or returned to the laws of the Scriptures to follow the laws of God exclusively. As a result of their lack of repentance, Israel suffered a succession of evil kings until both Israel and Judah were finally conquered by the Assyrians and Babylonians, respectively, centuries later.

As a consequence, the Jewish descendants of Menelik I of Ethiopia, the royal son of Solomon, did not return the Ark to Jerusalem. The descendants of Menelik I and his Jewish priests, advisors, and servants from the various tribes of Israel called themselves "Bet-Israel' (House of Israel) and ultimately grew to constitute a considerable portion of Ethiopia's northern population. They are called "Falasha" (exiles) by their neighbors.

These Ethiopian descendants of Israel formed the ruling class during thousands of years of Ethiopian history. The royal dynasty from Solomon and the Queen of Sheba ruled continuously until the twelfth century A.D. The Abyssinian royal chronicles record that the Jewish Ethiopian kingdom was ruled by Queen Judith about A.D. 950 and the dynasty continued for another two centuries. For several hundred years following a Muslim invasion in the twelfth century, the Muslims ruled most of Ethiopia, until the original Solomonic dynasty was re-established in 1558 by a Jewish king. This Ethiopian-Jewish dynasty continued until the communist coup and death of Emperor Haile Selassie in 1975.

Some have asked how the Ark could exist in Ethiopia when Revelation 11:19 refers to the prophet John seeing the Ark of the Testimony in his vision of heaven. However, the Scriptures record that Moses built the Ark of the Covenant after the pattern of the Ark in heaven (Exodus 25). Therefore, there is no contradiction between John's vision in Revelation of an Ark of the Covenant existing in heaven and the earthly Ark of the Covenant being located in Ethiopia.

The Church of Zion of Mary

Deep within a complex of underground passages far beneath the ancient Church of Zion of Mary in Aksum in northern Ethiopia is a secret passage that leads to a highly guarded hiding place for the most sacred object in human history. For three thousand years, from the time of King Solomon, royal priestly guards of the ancient Ethiopian Jewish monarchy protected this passage to the Holy of Holies.

Within this underground temple are seven concentric rings of interior circular walls. An ordinary Ethiopian Coptic priest can worship within the areas of the first to the fourth outermost rings. Only the highest priests and the emperor can enter the fifth and sixth innermost rings. The final, innermost seventh ring forms a walled circular room. It is the secret Holy of Holies. Only one person is allowed to enter this room; he is called the Guardian of the Ark. This Ethiopian priest-guard is chosen at the age of seven, the age of understanding, from the main priestly family. He is trained as a child, in his age of innocence, and agrees to guard the Ark for the rest of his life. This individual gives up the freedom of a normal life. As the Guardian of the Ark, he fasts for 225 days every year according to the Ethiopian Jewish sacred festival calendar. He prays, meditates, and guards the sacred Ark with his life. He never leaves this Holy of Holies until the day of his death, when he is replaced by another chosen Guardian. Each day the high priest enters the sixth innermost ring to bring the Guardian food and verify the Ark's safety.

The altars and communion tables of both ancient and modern Christian churches in Ethiopia contain a wooden carving of the Ark of the Covenant, called the Tabot (the Holy Ark-Ge'ez), which symbolizes that the ancient Ark is still in their midst. Several news articles also have referred to the location of the Ark. The Jewish magazine, *B'nai B'rith Messenger*, reported the following in 1935:

> The Tablets of the Law received by Moses on Mount Sinai and the Ark of the Covenant, both said to have been brought to Ethiopia from Jerusalem by Menelik, the son

of King Solomon and the Queen of Sheba, who was the founder of the present Abyssinian dynasty, have been removed to the mountain strongholds of Abyssinia for safekeeping because of the impending Italian invasion, according to word received here from Addis Ababa, the capital of Ethiopia.[6]

Canada's largest newspaper, the *Toronto Star*, dated July 19, 1981, included the following information:

In July 1936, a news service reported from Paris that a Semitic syndicate had approached French underwriters about insuring the Ark—said by the dispatch to be in Ethiopia—against war damage. The report explained that "the oblong, coffin-like chest of acacia wood, overlaid with gold within and without, was carried in ancient times as a protection against the enemy. It was believed that the Ethiopians, with their Semitic tradition and ancestry, might again bring it forth. This time it would be in the midst of tanks, airplanes, and machine guns instead of spear-bearing bowman as recorded in the Old Testament.[7]

In May 1948, word spread among the Jews of Ethiopia that Israel had declared itself an independent nation. Many of the "Falashas" began converging to the capital to discuss plans to return to Israel and help with the prophesied rebuilding of the Temple. Over the last fifty years, thousands of Ethiopian Jews have trickled back to Israel. However, Israel only officially admitted the "Falashas" into Israel as legitimate Jews under their "Law of Return" beginning in 1989.

From the rebirth of Israel in 1948, the Jewish government enjoyed very close relations with Emperor Haile Selassie and supplied considerable technical support and financial aid to Ethiopia. Members of the royal family have told me that Israeli government representatives helped Ethiopia on many occasions and that Israeli agents repeatedly asked the emperor about the Ark of the Covenant in Aksum. These Jewish diplomatic agents suggested that, since Israel had returned from captivity to become a strong nation and had recaptured the Temple Mount in 1967, the time had come for the Ethiopians to return the Ark to its ancient resting place in a rebuilt Temple in Jerusalem. The emperor is reported to have replied, "In principle, I agree that the Ark should be returned to the Temple, but the correct time has not yet come" (personal conversation with Prince Stephen Mengesha). He felt that God would reveal the right time to return the Ark to Jerusalem. Tragically, the Marxist army coup killed the emperor in 1975, devastated the nation economically, and led Ethiopia into a brutal civil war that finally ended in 1991.

In 1988, as the Eritrean rebel armies advanced from the north, Israel made an agreement with the leaders of the corrupt Marxist Ethiopian government to begin a partial rescue of the thousands of endangered Ethiopian Jews from the northern provinces of the country. In return for allowing this rescue of the Falasha Jews, Israel would supply desperately needed technical and financial aid. In 1991, Israel launched an extraordinary rescue operation, known as Operation Solomon, during the chaotic final days of the Ethiopian civil war. This rescue mission flew tens of thousands of Ethiopian Jews to the ancient homeland that their forefathers had left three thousand years earlier. The military leaders of Ethiopia's collapsing Communist govern-ment demanded and received millions of dollars in bribes from Israel during the final months of the war for permitting Israel to rescue these persecuted Ethiopian Jews. Israel flew numerous military cargo flights into the Ethiopian capital, Addis Ababa, to gather these destitute people who had fled to the capital to escape the growing persecution in their traditional homeland in the northern province of Gonder. After a great deal of research, debate, and counsel, the two chief rabbis of Israel accepted the Falasha as legitimate Jews who were separated from the twelve tribes in the ancient past.

A Secret Mission: Return the Ark to Israel

In the years following this dramatic Israeli rescue of the Ethiopian Jews, I interviewed three individuals who were knowledgeable about the details of a secret mission carried out during the chaotic closing days of the civil war in 1991. Two of my military sources, one an Ethiopian and one an Israeli, personally knew participants in the extraordinary rescue mission to bring the Ark home to Jerusalem. My third source was the Honorable Robert N. Thompson, an experienced retired Canadian diplomat and former member of Canada's Parliament. Thompson traveled to Ethiopia during the final days of the civil war in an audacious and successful attempt to rescue the surviving princes and princesses of the Ethiopian royal family, who had endured brutal imprisonment for fourteen years under the Communist dictator. I have known Thompson since I was a young boy and have admired his incredible career as a Canadian military officer in Ethiopia in World War II, a missionary, a member of Parliament, a leader of a conservative political party in Canada, and a diplomat serving as Canada's ambassador to NATO. In the years following World War II, Thompson served as a senior advisor and friend to Emperor Haile Selassie, assisting in the creation of Ethiopia's education and health care systems. He is the godfather of Prince Mengesha.

During his visit to my parents' home when I was a young boy, Robert Thompson told me that the true Ark of the Covenant was held in Aksum, Ethiopia. Following his return from the rescue of the surviving members of the royal family in Ethiopia, and shortly before his death I had the opportunity to discuss these events with Thompson at his home in British Columbia. He revealed to me that his Ethiopian sources had disclosed to him other details that confirmed the story I now relate regarding the rescue of the Ark of the Covenant.

All three of my sources confirmed essentially the same account: During the final days of the civil war, negotiations about the release of the Ark of the Covenant in Aksum took place between Israel's Mossad agents and the Ethiopian generals. The Ethiopian military leaders demanded a bribe of 42 million dollars to allow the Ark to be taken home to Israel. A number of wealthy Jewish families donated the necessary funds. Several large suitcases containing the ransom money were delivered to the corrupt government officials, who promptly deserted their posts in Ethiopia to fly with their loot to Switzerland. However, unknown to the departing officials, the suitcases contained counterfeit U.S. dollars. The Israeli agents promptly phoned the banks in Switzerland to inform them of the worthless counterfeit currency these Ethiopian officials were trying to deposit. Israel then took the millions raised by their Jewish donors and gave it to the new Ethiopian government that had just conquered the capital of Addas Ababa. Since the outgoing officials had looted the country's treasury, these millions of dollars from Israel were desperately needed and appreciated by the new, struggling democratic government as they attempted to reconstruct their country after years of mismanagement by the Communists.

I was informed by the same sources, that a special team of young Israeli soldiers flew an unmarked Israeli military cargo plane into the northern province of Gonder and secretly entered the sacred city of Aksum at night during the closing days of the civil war. Each one of these Israeli special forces soldiers were handpicked, descended from the tribe of Levi.

According to the law of Moses, only trained Levites were to carry the Ark of the Covenant (Numbers 4:15). Jews who have the surname Levi or Cohen (Kohanim, "sons of Aaron") are the only ones who can be certain of their tribal identity as Levites. According to my sources, these specially trained men, accompanied by Israeli elite special forces, secretly removed the Ark from the underground Holy of Holies in the deep complex of tunnels beneath the Church of Zion of Mary in Aksum. They carried the Ark, with its special blue covering, into the military cargo plane using the staves to carry it on their shoulders, in the biblically prescribed manner. After arriving in Israel, the Ark was taken to a secure and secret repository near Jerusalem, where it will be held until the divinely appointed time comes to put it in its proper place within the Holy of Holies of a rebuilt Temple. A source close to Israel's Chief Rabbi confirmed that Israel is now in possession of the Ark.

Obviously, the nature of this event means that these reports are impossible to document. However, the three people who gave me this information are credible, and the facts related are consistent with other details that I have discovered.

Other Suggested Locations of the Ark

Many Christian and Jewish scholars believe that the true Ark of the Covenant never left Israel. For example, there are Jewish traditional legends from the books of the Apocrypha such as the second book of Maccabees that relate that the prophet Jeremiah secretly hid the Tabernacle, the Ark, and the altar of incense in a cave in Mount Pisgah in Jordan before the Babylonians burned Solomon's Temple.

> The prophet, being warned of God, commanded the tabernacle and the ark to go with him, as he went forth into the mountain, where Moses climbed up, and saw the heritage of God. And when Jeremy came thither, he found an hollow cave, wherein he laid the tabernacle, and the ark, and the altar of incense, and so stopped the door. And some of those that followed him came to mark the way, but they could not find it. Which when Jeremy perceived, he blamed them, saying, As for that place, it shall be unknown until the time that God gather his people again together, and receive them unto mercy. Then shall the Lord shew them these things, and the glory of the Lord shall appear, and the cloud also, as it was shewed under Moses, and as when Solomon desired that the place might be honourably sanctified. (2 Maccabees 2:4–8)

However, this story includes many elements that are unlikely, including the fact that it claims that the Ark, altar of incense, and Tabernacle floated in the air behind the prophet as he traveled over twenty-five miles to Jordan's Mount Pisgah.

Other theories have suggested Jewish rebels took the Ark to Masada in A.D. 70. This theory is contradicted by the fact that the Jewish *Mishna* commentary states clearly that the Ark was not in the Second Temple. An amateur archeologist, Ron Wyatt, claimed that he discovered the Ark hidden under Calvary, the place of Christ's crucifixion, near the Garden Tomb. He produced a video that claims he found the true Ark. After three interviews with Wyatt prior to his death and several interviews with volunteers who assisted him, I have concluded that his claim is totally unfounded. The people in charge of the Garden Tomb where he conducted his investigation absolutely dismiss his claims. Jesus was crucified at Calvary, the ancient place of execution in Jerusalem. This site of death and execution of criminals was the most spiritually defiled place in Jerusalem in the mind of religious Jews. The suggestion that the Jewish priests charged with protecting the Ark would choose to hide their most sacred possession, the true Ark of the Covenant, under the spiritually defiled place of execution of criminals is simply not credible.

Other writers have suggested that the Ark is still hidden in one of the secret tunnels or chambers located underneath the Temple Mount. The *Talmud* refers to a tradition that King Solomon constructed a hidden room to hide the Ark from future invaders. The tradition suggests that the Jewish priests hid the Ark during the siege in 587 B.C. when the Babylonian army of King Nebuchadnezzar conquered the Holy Sanctuary. One source told me in confidence that he as well as Jewish archeologists and Rabbi Getz, the rabbi of the Western Wall, believed they saw an object, possibly the Ark of the Covenant, at a distance of approximately fifty yards in one of these tunnels but were prevented from approaching it because they feared to violate the sanctity of the Holy of Holies. However, the Muslim authorities in charge of the Temple Mount immediately sealed up the tunnel entrance, preventing any further examination. In the light of the historical evidence and the prophetic Scriptures already quoted, the object observed in the tunnel under the Temple Mount may either be the replica ark originally made for Prince Menelik I or possibly some other Temple object of worship such as the altar of incense. It also could have been a quantity of illegal weapons hidden under a tarp by Palestinian terrorists, as a Palestinian source suggested.

Whether the true Ark of the Covenant was returned from Ethiopia or will be found in a secret repository under the Temple Mount, the Bible indicates that the Ark still has a significant role to play in the final events of this age.

The Future of the Ark of the Covenant

Does Bible prophecy reveal anything about the location and the future of the Ark? In the great prophecy of Ezekiel (38–39) about the coming War of Gog and Magog, he describes the supernatural defeat of the invading armies of the Russian and the Arab nations. The prophet then reports that God will set up an object of worship ("my glory") that both the Gentile nations and Israel will recognize as proof that God has once again intervened in history to save His chosen people.

The prophet Ezekiel declared, "And I will set my glory among the heathen, and all the heathen shall see my judgment that I have executed, and my hand that I have laid upon them. So the house of Israel shall know that I am the Lord their God from that day and forward" (Ezekiel 39:21–22).

One final prophecy provides, perhaps, the strongest evidence that the Ark will be recovered and play an important role in our future. The prophet Jeremiah describes a time after the Battle of Armageddon has been won when the Messiah rules and Israel is enjoying its messianic kingdom:

> And it shall come to pass, when ye be multiplied and increased in the land, in those days, saith the Lord, they shall say no more, The Ark of the Covenant of the Lord: neither shall it come to mind: neither shall they remember it; neither shall they visit it; neither shall that be done any more. At that time they shall call Jerusalem the throne of the Lord; and all the nations shall be gathered unto it, to the name of the Lord, to Jerusalem. (Jeremiah 3: 16–17)

In other words, Jeremiah prophesied that once the Messiah wins the Battle of Armageddon and sets up His millennial kingdom, the people of Israel will stop talking about the Ark, they will stop thinking about the Ark, and they will stop visiting the Ark. The reason the Ark of the Covenant and its Shekinah glory will no longer be the focus of the worship of the people of Israel is that Jesus Christ Himself will be present to be worshiped directly as their Messiah-King and God.

However, consider the fact that Jews have not publicly talked about, thought about, or visited the Ark of the Covenant for almost three thousand years since it disappeared during the days of King Solomon, approximately 980 B.C. This prophecy of Jeremiah 3:16–17 implies that the lost Ark of the Covenant will be rediscovered and will play a pivotal role in the spiritual life of Israel during the prophetic events of the last days.

If the tentative suggestions of this chapter are correct, the recovery of the lost Ark and its subsequent role in Israel's miraculous victory in the War of Gog and Magog would encourage the Jews to begin the rebuilding of their Temple. The return of the Ark of the Covenant to the Holy of Holies of a rebuilt Temple would signal for Israel the beginning of the long-awaited messianic era.

Notes

1. Grant R. Jeffrey, *The Signature of God* (Toronto: Frontier Research Publications, Inc., 1996).
2. David Lewis, *Prophecy 2000* (Green Forest, Arizona: New Lea Press, 1990).
3. Arthur Bloomfield, *End of the Days* (Bloomington: Bethany House Publishers, 1998).
4. Leo Roberts, *National Geographic*, 1935.
5. "Ethiopia," *Encyclopædia Britannica*, 1970 edition.
6. "Ark of the Covenant," *B'nai B'rith Messenger*, 1935.
7. *Toronto Sun* 19 July 1981.

11

Jonah and the Great Fish

One of the greatest mysteries in the Bible is the amazing story about the prophet Jonah, who tried to escape from the missionary journey to Nineveh that God called him to perform. When the sailors threw him into the sea to quell a storm, Jonah was swallowed by a great fish and was thrown out on the shore after "three days and three nights." For many people, this biblical account appears to be simply impossible, and they have concluded that it must be a myth. However, a careful reading of the Scriptures reveals a very factual account of the remarkable event. The Old Testament book of Jonah records: "The Lord had prepared a great fish to swallow up Jonah. And Jonah was in the belly of the fish three days and three nights." (Jonah 1:17). In the New Testament Jesus Christ stated to His disciples that He (Jesus Christ) would be three days and three nights in the heart of the earth, just as Jonah was "three days and three nights in the whale's belly" (Matthew 12:40.)

The question all readers must confront is this: Are we to

understand the account of Jonah and the great fish literally as an historical account? Or are we to interpret this biblical story as a simple myth or symbolic truth that is not based on the historic truthfulness of the underlying story?

Skeptics usually reject the story of Jonah and the great fish out of hand on the basis that they believe no known sea creature could possibly swallow a man whole, and the survival of such a man for several days is simply beyond the realm of possibility or of human experience. However, the research documented later in this chapter reveals that both these assumptions are false.

Is the Book of Jonah an Historical Account or a Myth?

The first thing to note is that Jonah is clearly a historical figure mentioned in other biblical documents. Secondly, the style of the book of Jonah is a normal historical narrative. Thirdly, until relatively recently, the vast majority of Christian and Jewish scholars and laypeople accepted the reality of Jonah and his

Jonah Cast Into Sea. Painting by Nicolas Poussin.

ministry to Nineveh. Finally, Jesus Christ Himself repeatedly testified to the historical truthfulness of Jonah's experience.

The first biblical reference to Jonah as a real person is found in the historical books of the Old Testament that record Jonah's ministry as a prophet. "He [King Jeroboam of Israel] restored the coast of Israel from the entering of Hamath unto the sea of the plain, according to the word of the Lord God of Israel, which he spake by the hand of his servant Jonah, the son of Amittai, the prophet, which was of Gathhepher" (2 Kings 14: 25). The biblical book of Jonah recorded the entire account of the divine call to ministry, the supernatural experience with the great fish, his ministry, and the miraculous repentance of the Ninevites in response to Jonah's prophetic warning of God's coming judgment.

Jesus Himself referred to Jonah and this miracle as a historical event, and He stated that this event foreshadowed His own death and resurrection. Two of the Gospels record Jesus' words about the ministry of Jonah. In the book of Matthew, Jesus spoke of Jonah as a real person. "But he answered and said unto them, An evil and adulterous generation seeketh after a sign; and there shall no sign be given to it, but the sign of the prophet Jonas [Jonah]: For as Jonas was three days and three nights in the whale's belly; so shall the Son of man be three days and three nights in the heart of the earth. The men of Nineveh shall rise in judgment with this generation, and shall condemn it: because they repented at the preaching of Jonas; and, behold, a greater than Jonas is here" (Matthew 12:39–41). Later, in Matthew 16:4, Jesus again referred to Jonah's miraculous delivery as the "sign of the prophet Jonas." Christ warned, "A wicked and adulterous generation seeketh after a sign; and there shall no sign be given unto it, but the sign of the prophet Jonas. And he left them, and departed" (Matthew 16:4). The gospel of Luke also records Christ's words identifying Jonas as a historical person (Luke 11:29–30, 32).

Clearly, these references to Jonah by Jesus Christ provide powerful evidence that the prophet was a historical person and that the fascinating account of his miraculous survival within the stomach of the great fish is true. In fact, Jesus compared

Jonah's experience with the great fish to the literal truth of His resurrection from the dead after "three days and three nights." For those Christians who accept that Jesus is the Son of God, it is inconceivable that He could be mistaken in His identification of Jonah as a real person if this was only a myth or symbolic story.

The manner in which the writer of the book of Jonah has written his account strongly suggests that he expects the reader to accept the story at face value as a historical event. One of the problems is that modern skeptics, who automatically reject any miraculous or supernatural accounts as impossible, reject the very possibility that the story of Jonah and the great fish could be true. However, if we wish to objectively arrive at a true and balanced understanding of this strange account, we must be willing to examine the available evidence from historical, archeological, scriptural, and scientific sources. This section will examine all of the available evidence to arrive at the truth regarding the mystery of Jonah and his strange experience.

Historical and Archeological Evidence Supporting the Ministry of the Prophet

Despite the fact that many people believe that the whole account of Jonah and the great fish is a pure myth without historical accuracy, the truth is that there is ample historical, archaeological, and scriptural evidence that supports the credibility of the biblical account as recorded in both Old and New Testament references to the ministry of the prophet Jonah and this miraculous event.

Archeologists have uncovered the ancient ruins of the city of Nineveh and have proven that it was an enormous city during biblical times. To their surprise, the archaeologists have discovered numerous statutes and bas-relief clay engravings that recorded the prominent position of a pagan deity in ancient Assyria known as Dagan. This remarkable pagan god was depicted as being a creature that was partly a man and partly a fish. Occasionally Dagan was represented in Assyrian art as a figure standing upright possessing the head of a fish above a human head. Often the depiction revealed the fish with an open mouth forming the image of a miter as part of the human's sacred headdress. The feet of a man usually extended below the tail of the fish. Occasionally, the body of a man was depicted at right angles to the upright body of the fish. Archeologists discovered images of the fish-god Dagan in the ancient city of Nineveh, usually at the entrance to the palace and temple. Images of Dagan also are found on many ancient Babylonian seals.

The ancient Babylonian historian Berosus, who wrote during the fourth century B.C., recorded the early traditions revealing the origin of the Assyrian worship of this fish-man. Remarkably, the earliest tradition indicates that a divine being, partly man and partly fish, rose from the sea and created the new civilization in Chaldea and Babylonia. At the very time of Jonah's ministry to Nineveh, the Assyrian people believed that their deity sent them messages through a special being, Dagan, who rose out of the sea, appearing in the form of a fish-man. This widespread tradition helps explain why the pagans of Nineveh would have been especially willing to listen to the divine message by the Israelite prophet Jonah once they realized that he had been swallowed and then vomited out of a fish.

The name Dagan is found quite often in the earliest Assyrian records. The Babylonian historian Berosus recorded the name of the Assyrian fish-god as "Oannes." Some have speculated that Oannes is actually a reference to the ministry of Jonah, due to his obvious connection with their ancient myth of the fish-god. It is interesting to note that both the Greek translation of the Old Testament, the Septuagint, and the New Testament Greek text spell the name Jonah as Oannes with the addition of the letter *I* before it (*Ioannes*). The eminent Assyriologist Dr. Herman V. Hilprecht revealed that in the Assyrian inscriptions the letter *J* in foreign words is often written as *I*, or is dropped completely. Therefore, the Greek name of Jonah, *Joannes*, would be rendered in Assyrian inscriptions as either *Ioannes* or *Oannes*. According to Hilprecht, the Greek or Babylonian rendition for Jonah would be *Oannes*.[1]

Another fascinating discovery is that the inscriptions in the ruins of Nineveh contain several clear references to the name "Yunas," or "Jonah." The preservation of these names supports the historicity of the biblical account of Jonah's ministry. The archeologists discovered the famed elaborate palaces of the ancient kings of Assyria beneath the earthen mound in the ruins of Nineveh that was known to the surrounding Arab villages for centuries as "Neby Yunas."[2]

H. Clay Trumbull wrote of Jonah's ministry in the *Journal of Biblical Literature* in 1892 as follows: "What better heralding, as a divinely sent messenger to Nineveh, could Jonah have had, than to be thrown up out of the mouth of a great fish, in the presence of witnesses, say, on the coast of Phoenicia, where the fish-god was a favorite object of worship? . . . The recorded sudden and profound alarm of the people of an entire city at his warning was most natural, as a result of the coincidence of this miracle with their religious beliefs and expectations."[3]

A Whale or a Great Fish?

The Hebrew text of the Old Testament used the Hebrew word *dag gadol* which means "great fish," as opposed to a specific word for a whale. Dr. Gleason Archer wrote in his book, *A Survey of Old Testament Introduction*, that Hebrew had no specific word identifying a whale.[4] The Greek New Testament word translated into English as "whale" in Matthew is actually the word for a "huge fish" that could either be a fish or a whale. James Strong's *Dictionary of the Words in the Greek New Testament* reveals that the Greek word translated "whale" is *ketos* (pronounced kay-tos), and it means "a huge fish (as gaping for prey)." The Scriptures affirm that God "prepared a great fish to swallow up Jonah." This account reveals that the Lord supernaturally arranged this sea creature to be there to fulfill His plan to discipline His disobedient prophet, Jonah. Since scientists had not yet identified the taxonomic differences between great fish and the mammal known today as the whale, the seventy translators who created the King James Version of the Bible in 1611 naturally chose the word "whale" to describe the largest sea creature known to them at that time.

Could a Whale or Great Fish Swallow a Man Whole?

It is important to recognize that the account of a whale or great fish swallowing Jonah and vomiting him out alive after a few days is extremely unusual, but it is not impossible. Several huge sea creatures, including sperm whales, blue whales, whale sharks, and great white sharks, grow to such enormous size that they could indeed swallow a man whole. In addition, there are several authenticated historical accounts of individuals being swallowed by such sea creatures and surviving to tell the tale.

The *Daily Mail* newspaper reported on December 14, 1928, the testimony of Mr. G. H. Henn, a resident of Birmingham, England: "My own experience was in Birmingham about 25 years ago, when the carcass of a whale was displayed for a week. . . . I was one of twelve men who went into its mouth, passed through its throat, and moved about in what was equivalent to a fair-sized room. Its throat was large enough to serve as a door. Obviously it would be quite easy for a whale of this kind to swallow a man."[5]

The late Sir Francis Fox wrote a book entitled *Sixty-three Years of Engineering*. Fox wrote that the manager of a whaling station recorded that a sperm whale can swallow lumps of food up to eight feet wide. In one case when they examined a large whale, they found "the skeleton of a shark sixteen feet in length!"[6] Richard M. Riss has accumulated excellent research regarding the historical parallels with biblical account of Jonah and the great fish. I recommend his Web site on Christian Evidences: http://www.grmi.org/renewal/Richard_Riss/evidences/8jonah.html.

There are two documented historical accounts of people who were swallowed by whales and large fish and then survived the remarkable experience:

A Sailor Survived Being Swallowed by an Enormous Fish

A huge species, the great white shark (*Carcharodon carcharias*), which reaches a length of twenty-one feet, exists in most warm oceans. In 1758, a sailor fell overboard from a boat in the Mediterranean and was swallowed by a great white shark. The captain ordered his sailors to fire a deck cannon at the huge sea creature, which was still on the surface of the water. The huge shark vomited up the sailor. Remarkably, the sailor was still alive and unharmed.[7]

Marshall Jenkins, A.D. 1771

There is another report of a man, Marshall Jenkins, surviving after being ingested by a huge sperm whale during a whale hunt in the South Seas during the fall of 1771. As the *Boston Post Boy* newspaper reported on October 14, 1771, a whaling vessel from the port of Edgartown, Massachusetts harpooned a sperm whale that turned and attacked its pursuers. First, the whale bit into one of the boats, breaking it into two parts. Then, the whale swallowed the sailor Marshall Jenkins and submerged beneath the ocean's surface with him in its stomach. When the enormous whale finally rose again to the surface, the whale vomited Jenkins onto the floating wreckage of the broken harpoon boat, "much bruised but not seriously injured."[8]

Conclusion

The evidence strongly supports the historical truth of the biblical account of Jonah and the great fish. Since the Bible tells us that God "prepared the great fish," we can conclude that either the Lord specially created a sea creature for this purpose or that He caused an existing huge sea creature to be in the right place at the right time to swallow Jonah and later release him. In either case, the evidence we have documented in this section reveals that the biblical account is a credible historical account of God's merciful dealing with His prophet Jonah and the people of the ancient city of Nineveh.

Notes

1. H. Clay Trumbull, "Jonah in Nineveh," *Journal of Biblical Literature* 11 (1892) 14.
2. H. Clay Trumbull, "Jonah in Nineveh," *Journal of Biblical Literature* 11 (1892)17–18.
3. H. Clay Trumbull, "Jonah in Nineveh," *Journal of Biblical Literature* 11 (1892) 10–12.
4. Gleason Archer, Jr., *A Survey of Old Testament Introduction*, revised edition, (Chicago: Moody Press, 1974) 314.
5. *Daily Mail* 14 Dec. 1928.
6. Quoted in Ambrose John Wilson, "The Sign of the Prophet Jonah and Its Modern Confirmations," *The Princeton Theological Review* 25 (1927) 636.
7. Ambrose John Wilson, "The Sign of the Prophet Jonah and Its Modern 8. 8. Confirmations," *The Princeton Theological Review* 25 (1927) 638, footnote 20.
8. Ambrose John Wilson, "The Sign of the Prophet Jonah and Its Modern Confirmations," *The Princeton Theological Review* 25 (1927): 636–637.

12

Joshua's Long Day

Among the hundreds of biblical mysteries that millions have pondered over the centuries, the mystery concerning the unusually long day recorded in the book of Joshua has puzzled more people than most other biblical questions. From the standpoint of astronomy, it is virtually impossible for a scientist, even a conservative Christian astronomer, to imagine how God supernaturally arranged things to extend the day's sunlight during the battle in the Valley of Ajalon to allow Joshua's army the extra hours they needed to totally defeat their Canaanite enemies.

Although numerous theories, some fascinating and others absurd, have been proposed over the years, my Christian associates who are knowledgeable about astronomy assure me that there are as yet no credible theories to explain the astronomical phenomenon described in the book of Joshua. As a Christian who has learned to trust the Word of God, I accept that Joshua's account is the truth. For one thing, it is inconceivable that the book of Joshua's account of the long day would have been accepted as biblical truth by the ancient Jews if this miraculous event had not actually occurred in the not-too-distant past.

Then spake Joshua to the Lord in the day when the Lord delivered up the Amorites before the children of Israel, and he said in the sight of Israel, Sun, stand thou still upon Gibeon; and thou, Moon, in the valley of Ajalon. And the sun stood still, and the moon stayed, until the people had avenged themselves upon their enemies. Is not this written in the book of Jasher? So the sun stood still in the midst of heaven, and hasted not to go down about a whole day. And there was no day like that before it or after it, that the Lord hearkened unto the voice of a man: for the Lord fought for Israel. (Joshua 10:12–14)

Some critics have objected to the biblical account on the basis that the scriptural language states that "the sun . . . hasted not to go down." They argue that this geocentric language refers to the sun as if it orbited around the earth rather than the scientific reality that the earth orbits around the sun. However, this criticism is invalid because the Bible simply used the normal language

The War Against Gibeon. Painting by Gustave Doré.

of appearance that all of us use in our everyday language to describe events as they appear to us. For example, scientists discussing weather phenomena still commonly refer to "sunrise" and "sunset," although they are naturally aware that the sun does not rise in the morning or set in the evening. It only appears that way from the standpoint of a human observer on earth and is therefore naturally described that way in ordinary language.

The Historical Context

The book of Joshua records that five pagan kings launched a war against the Gibeonites, the nearby people who had tricked Israel into entering into a treaty of mutual defense. The pagan alliance included the six kings of the Amorites, Jerusalem, Hebron, Jarmuth, Lachish, and Eglon, who massed their armies to destroy Gibeon. When the Gibeonites begged the Israelites for assistance, Joshua prepared the army to assist in the defense of their ally. God promised Joshua that He would defeat the enemies of Israel. When Joshua asked the Lord to give Israel's army additional hours of sunlight to enable them to fully defeat their enemy, God responded with a remarkable miracle that is unprecedented in human history.

It is worthwhile to note that the biblical account implies that Joshua called upon God to extend the hours of daylight after noon. Why would anyone call for extra hours of sunlight if it were still morning? From noon until dusk was a duration of approximately seven hours. Yet the Bible records that Joshua's army pursued the armies of the six kings from Gibeon to Makkedah (Joshua 10:10), a distance of twenty-seven miles. Military historians note that the most a large land army can march in one complete day of twelve to fourteen hours is twenty-five to thirty miles. Therefore, the fact that the Israelites pursued their enemies for twenty-seven miles and then observed the hanging of the pagan kings at the cave near Makkedah before "the going down of the sun" strongly supports the account that God supernaturally extended the hours of light to allow the Israelites to utterly defeat their enemies.

Scientific Explanations

The various theories that have been proposed to describe how God accomplished this miracle of the long day tend to fall into three categories.

A Refraction of the Sun's and Moon's Light

The first approach is to assume that God used some form of refraction (bending) of the light from the sun and the moon. In effect, supporters of this theory propose that the Lord somehow miraculously extended the sunlight as well as the moonlight by refraction to enable the Israelites to defeat their enemies without actually altering the orbits of the sun, moon, or earth. This theory avoids the problems of changing orbits and also focuses on Joshua's need for additional hours of light as opposed to needing a change in the orbits of celestial bodies. Supporters of this theory also point to the likelihood that some type of refraction of light appears to be what is described in the supernatural account of the shadow going back ten degrees on King Ahaz's sundial as recorded in 2 Kings 20:11. The difficulty with this theory is that no one has successfully explained how the bending of the light would have been accomplished.

A Change in the Earth's Axis of Rotation

A second approach is to assume that God supernaturally caused a change or variation in the direction of the earth's axis of rotation. The theory suggests that there was a precession of the earth's axis in which it would wobble, slowly tracing a curved or circular path in the sky. They conclude that such an event would cause the appearance that the sun and moon had stopped their orbit for a number of hours. However, this would not involve any change or slowing of the sun's, moon's, or earth's rotations.

A Slowing of the Rotation of the Earth

This theory suggests that God supernaturally slowed the rotation of the earth as it orbited the sun to extend the hours of daylight. While this slowdown of the earth's rotation would have extended the daylight in accordance with the biblical account, it would have produced enormous additional problems that would have necessitated other supernatural interventions by God to prevent a violent planetary catastrophe. If God stopped or slowed the rotation of the earth, or changed the sun's orbit around the hub of our galaxy, the results would be catastrophic, including monstrous tidal waves, unless at the same time He supernaturally countered the massive effects of such a change in rotation or orbit.

If this is what occurred, then God would have needed to supernaturally slow the rotation of the earth's atmosphere and oceans at the same time that He slowed the earth's rotation to avoid massive tidal waves. Another factor is the simultaneous need to supernaturally slow the rotation of the molten core of the planet that is also rotating far beneath the earth's crust. Once Israel's battle was won, God would have needed to reverse the supernatural process to return the earth to its normal rotation. Some have suggested that if the earth's rotation slowed or stopped, then everything would fly off the ground. However, the force of gravity is approximately three hundred times more powerful than the centrifugal force caused by the earth's rotation, so objects would not fly into space if the earth's rotation slowed. Many have heard a story that claims scientists at NASA have calculated that there is a "missing day" in the earth's history that corresponds to Joshua's long day. However, this story is false and has been denied by NASA officials.

The fact is that we are still at a loss at the present time to determine scientifically exactly how God accomplished the mysterious miracle known as Joshua's long day.

The account of Joshua's long day cannot be astronomically confirmed at this time due to a lack of essential scientific data regarding (1) the exact date and time of Creation; (2) the date of the Joshua event itself; and (3) the precise orbital characteristics of all relevant celestial bodies, most especially the sun, earth, and moon, both at the time of Creation and immediately preceding the Joshua event.

Historical Accounts of the Sun Standing Still

However, there are numerous fascinating historical accounts of similar unusual solar and lunar phenomena in ancient times that were recorded by many other nations. These additional historical accounts of the sun and moon behaving in an extraordinary manner strongly suggest that the Bible's remarkable account that "the sun stood still, and the moon stayed" actually occurred. Obviously, the long day would also have had an impact on nations and peoples around the globe far from the land of Israel. If such a remarkable astronomical event truly occurred, it would inevitably have left an extraordinary historical memory of a day unlike any other in human history. It is my purpose in this section to examine several of these historical accounts of extremely unusual phenomena related to the sun and moon that may provide confirmation of Joshua's account.

The Historian Herodotus and the Egyptian Priests

The Greek historian Herodotus wrote in his *History* that Egyptian priests had reported a most unusual solar event that occurred in the distant past. "Thus the whole number of years [of early Egyptian history] is 341 pharaohs, in which entire space, they said, no god had ever appeared in a human form; nothing of this kind had happened either under the former or under the later Egyptian kings. The sun, however, had within this period of time, on four several occasions, moved from his wonted course, twice rising where he now sets, and twice setting where he now rises."[1]

The Greeks

The Greek poet Homer wrote about the mythic god Phaethon riding the chariot of the sun high up into the sky before losing control and crashing to earth. In Homer's *Iliad,* he wrote, "King Agamemnon raised his voice in prayer: 'Zeus, Zeus, god of greatness, god of glory, lord god of the dark clouds who lives in the bright sky, don't let the sun go down or the night descend on us!'"[2] The war that Homer wrote about occurred at approximately the same time as the events recorded in the book of Joshua. In Homer's *Odyssey,* he wrote about a time when the dawn was held back from appearing. "Indeed they would have gone on indulging their sorrow till rosy-fingered morn appeared, had not Minerva determined otherwise, and held night back in the far west, while she would not suffer Dawn to leave Oceanus."[3]

The Romans

The Roman writer Seneca reported in his drama *Thyestes:* "The sun reversed its course and blotted out the day in mid-Olympus [noon]." This appears to be a parallel account to the event described in the book of Joshua.[4]

The Aztecs

Aztec priests related to the Spanish scholar Bernardino de Sahagun (1499–1590) that the sun had acted in a most unusual way in the ancient past. The Aztecs were very sophisticated in their astronomical calculations and their amazingly precise ability to compute the solar calendar. Bernardino de Sahagun, who traveled to Mexico in the generation following Columbus's discovery of America, recorded this Aztec tradition: "And when the sun came to rise . . . he kept swaying from side to side . . . with a rabbit he came to wound in the face [the moon], and he killed its brilliance . . . when both appeared they could not move nor follow their paths. . . . At once he [the wind] could move him, who thereupon went his way. And when he had followed his course only the moon remained there."[5] Significantly, he also wrote that the Aztecs reported that at one point in ancient times both the sun and moon stood still shortly after sunrise.

The Mexicans

In the sixteenth-century Mexican text *Annals of Cuauhtitlan,* which records the history of the Culhuacan empire in ancient Mexico, there is a record of a night that extended far longer than normal.[6]

The Peruvians

There is also an ancient account of a day that lasted twice the normal time reported by Professor Olcot in his book exploring the history of the Peruvians.[7]

The Babylonians

Professor P. Jensen reported that the ancient Babylonians have an account of a "day of twice natural length."[8]

Conclusion

In conclusion, astronomers have not yet found any scientific evidence to confirm Joshua's account of the long day, nor can they provide a credible theory at this time of how God accomplished this miracle. However, the parallel accounts of similar extraordinary astronomical phenomena found in the records of many other nations provide compelling evidence that the biblical account that "the sun stood still, and the moon stayed" in the book of Joshua describes a mysterious but historically accurate event.

Notes

1. Herodotus, *The History of Herodotus*, trans. Chapter 2.
2. Homer, *The Iliad*, trans. 2:490.
3. Homer, *The Odyssey*, trans. 23
4. Seneca, *Thyestes*, Loeb Classical Library vol ix, trans. Frank J. Miller, 1917).
5. Bernardino de Sahagun, *Historia General de las Cosas de Nueva Espana*, 1946) VII: 2.
6. *Annals of Cuauhtitlan*, trans.
7. Olcot, *The Historical Lore of the Peruvians* (1914) 206.
8. P. Jensen, *Die Kosmologie der Babylonie*, trans. (Strassburg: 1890) 39.

13

Israel's Day of Tragedy – the Ninth Day of Av

There is a remarkable and unprecedented mystery in the history of the Jewish people that finds no parallel in the history of any other people. A strange and mysterious phenomenon of historical anniversaries has governed the life of the Chosen People that is remarkable and provides overwhelming evidence of the "hand of God" upon the events governing the life of the nation Israel.

Several years ago I wrote a book entitled *Armageddon – Appointment with Destiny* that explored this remarkable and previously unknown phenomenon that provided compelling evidence that God was controlling the events concerning the nation of the Jews.[1] For four thousand years, virtually every major event that affected the life of the nation Israel (over forty key events) fell on a precise day of the year on an exact festival or fast day that was commanded by God in the Exodus when the Jews escaped from centuries of bondage in Egypt. The book of Leviticus records that God commanded the people of Israel to eternally commemorate a series of festivals, feasts, and fasts that fell on the exact days of the ancient Jewish calendar when major supernatural events of the Exodus occurred during the life of Moses. "And Moses declared unto the children of Israel the feasts of the Lord" (Leviticus 23:44). God set these appointed "feasts of the Lord" for Israel to observe at specific times throughout the year (Leviticus 23). These feasts were to be celebrated from that time in the Exodus when God first gave the Law and were to continue on into the future. The following seven feasts in Leviticus 23 were to be celebrated annually: Passover, Unleavened Bread, Firstfruits, Pentecost, Trumpets, Atonement, and Tabernacles. Every single feast commemorated a specific historical event in the life of the Jewish nation.

However, from our present vantage point, I have discovered that numerous critical historical events have still occurred, after biblical times, on the exact days that God had instituted to commemorate the ancient biblical events. There are numerous anniversary historical events that I have documented in *Armageddon*. However, in this section I would like to explore the astonishing series of eight national disasters that occurred on one single day of the Jewish calendar. The odds against these eight national disasters occurring by random chance on the same day of the year are simply astonishing and virtually impossible.

The Ninth Day of the Jewish Month Av
The Fast of Mourning

The prophet Zechariah referred to this fast of mourning on the ninth day of the Jewish month of Av as follows: "When ye fasted and mourned in the fifth [Av] and seventh month" (Zechariah 7:5). This day of fasting, known as *Tisha B' Av*, is an extremely important day of mourning and remembrance in the religious life of the Jewish people; it commemorates Israel's tragic loss of the sacred Temple of Solomon in 587 B.C. This destruction of the Temple by the Babylonians is one of the most historically significant anniversaries in the life of Israel and is still commemorated by Jews worldwide as the tragic day when God withdrew His Shekinah glory. The ancient Jews wept as their precious Temple burned to the ground. The ninth of Av has become a day when Jews not only mourn their loss of the Temple but also look to that great day in the future when their Messiah will finally appear to end their centuries of suffering forever. Zechariah also stated that when the Messiah comes and sets up His long-promised Kingdom, then, all of their ancient fasts or mourning, including this one, will be transformed into feasts of joy. They "shall be to the house of Judah joy and gladness, and cheerful feasts (Zechariah 8:19).

Tisha B' Av, Israel's fast of mourning on the ninth day of Av, has seen more disasters than any other date in history. This phenomenon of eight major tragic historical disasters of the same nature all occurring on the same anniversary date is unprecedented in the history of the nations. Consider the historical evidence regarding these eight remarkable national disasters that fell on a single anniversary day over the course of many centuries.

1. The Twelve Spies in the Exodus Return with their Negative Report

Shortly after the successful escape from the armies of Pharaoh, Moses sent out the leaders of the twelve tribes to spy out the Promised Land forty days prior to the Jews entering the land of Canaan. However, due to unbelief in God's supernatural protection, ten of the twelve spies returned with pessimistic reports about how impossible it would be to conquer the Promised Land, even though God had promised them victory. The ancient Jewish commentary, the *Mishna*, records that the people believed the evil report, mourned all night in fear, and turned against Moses and the two faithful spies on the ninth day of the month Av (*Ta'anit* 29a) The result, according to Numbers 14:1–10, was a total rebellion, and it led to an attempt to stone Moses to death and return to the slavery of Egypt. If this rebellion against Moses' leadership had been successful, this violation of God's Covenant with Abraham would have led to the death and total assimilation of the Jewish people into Egypt.

Consequently, God judged the rebel leaders and warned the people of Israel that this sinful rebellion would result in that whole generation of the Exodus wandering in the wilderness of Sinai for forty years, even as the spies had searched out the land for forty days. The result of this awful rebellion and unbelief in

The Burning of Jerusalem. Painting by J. Goeree.

God's promises was the loss of the Promised Land for this entire generation, except for the two faithful spies, Joshua and Caleb. The Bible records that "Moses told these sayings unto all the children of Israel: and the people mourned greatly" (Numbers 14:39).

Thus, the ninth of Av became a fast of mourning as the Children of Israel wept over their lack of obedience to God, the prophecy of the death of that whole generation in the Sinai, and the tragedies that would follow repeatedly in the following centuries.

2. The Destruction of Solomon's Temple by the Babylonians

The Babylonian army under King Nebuchadnezzar besieged Jerusalem in 589 B.C. After a two-year siege they breached the walls and the Babylonian army directly attacked the Jews' final defenses on the massive Temple Mount.

According to the Jewish commentary *Me'am Lo'ez* and the *Jerusalem Talmud*, the Babylonian army fought their way into the Temple on the seventh day of Av, 587 B.C. "His men ate, drank and caroused there until the ninth of Av. Toward evening, they set the Temple on fire." The prophet Jeremiah, who was an eyewitness to the terrible destruction of the city, records that after the conquering of the city and the capture of King Zedekiah, the Temple was burned by the Babylonian captain of the guard, Nebuzaradan, and confirms that, with no attempts being made to fight the enormous fire, the huge Temple complex was still burning through until the next day, the tenth of Av (Jeremiah 52:5–14).

This tragedy has been commemorated ever since by a solemn fast on the ninth of Av, known as *Tisha B' Av*. For more than two thousand years, on this tragic day, the Jews have read the book of Lamentations in which Jeremiah mourns the destruction of Jerusalem and the loss of the great Temple of Solomon. "The Lord hath cast off his altar, he hath abhorred his sanctuary, he hath given up into the hand of the enemy the walls of the palaces; they have made a noise in the house of the Lord, as in the day of a solemn feast" (Lamentations 2:7; Zechariah 8:9).

3. The Destruction of the Second Temple by the Romans

The Romans went to war with the Jewish rebels beginning in A.D. 66, and their revolt was finally crushed by the Roman legions' destruction of their capital, Jerusalem, and their beloved Temple on the ninth day of Av in A.D. 70. Over 1.25 million people were trapped inside the city by the encircling Romans. On the ninth day of Av, the Romans reached the Temple compound. The Roman general, Titus, gave strict orders that the beautiful Temple, the greatest building in the Roman Empire, must not be destroyed. He implored the Jewish rebels to surrender on terms so that their great city and their sacred Temple would not be destroyed. However, the judgment of God was declared almost forty years earlier by Jesus Christ (Luke 19:41–44), and this terrible appointment with destiny could not be postponed. The Jewish rebel leaders rejected the offers of General Titus, and the desperate battle for the Temple Mount commenced. Despite the clear orders of Titus to the centurions, the enraged Roman soldiers threw their torches into the Temple and, within minutes, the Holy Place became an inferno. An eyewitness, the Jewish historian Flavius Josephus, reported that General Titus stood in the entrance to the Holy Place beating back his soldiers with his sword in a vain attempt to save at least the Inner Temple from their act of destruction.

Jesus Christ had warned thirty-eight years earlier, "For the days shall come upon thee, that thine enemies shall cast a trench about thee, and compass thee round, and keep thee in on every side, And shall lay thee even with the ground, and thy children within thee; and they shall not leave in thee one stone upon another; because thou knewest not the time of thy visitation" (Luke 19:43–44). When the Roman army burned the Temple, the tremendous heat of the fire melted the sheets of gold that covered much of the Temple building. The molten gold ran down into every crack between the foundation stones. When the fire finally died down, the Roman soldiers used wedges and crowbars to overturn every stone to search for this gold, thus fulfilling exactly Christ's prophetic words.

4. *The Roman Army Plowed Jerusalem and the Temple*

In A.D. 71, exactly one year after the Roman's destruction of Jerusalem and the Temple, on the ninth of Av, the Roman army plowed with salt the site of the Temple Mount and the whole city as a symbol of Rome's utter defeat of its enemy. This was a complete fulfillment of the prophecy of Micah: "Therefore shall Zion for your sakes be plowed as a field, and Jerusalem shall become heaps, and the mountain of the house as the high places of the forest" (Micah 3:12). The Jewish rabbinical source *Ta'anit* 26b records that the act was completed in preparation of making the city into a Roman colony known as *Aelia Capitolina.*

5. The Destruction of Simon Bar Cochba's Army

After the fall of Jerusalem, there was a period of enforced peace. Among those false prophets was a dynamic Jewish leader named Simon Bar Cochba. As Jesus had predicted, many people, including the famous Jewish scholar Rabbi Akiba, acclaimed him as the Messiah. Jesus prophesied before His rejection: "I am come in my Father's name, and ye receive me not; if another shall come in his own name, him ye will receive" (John 5:43). How sad that after rejecting the true Messiah they would now accept a counterfeit.

For two years Simon Bar Cochba and his followers were successful in repelling the Romans. Finally, Emperor Hadrian came with an enormous army that attacked and destroyed the Jewish rebels at Beitar, southwest of Jerusalem. On that tragic ninth of Av, A.D. 135, the last great army of an independent ancient Israel was slaughtered without mercy by the Roman legions. Dio Cassius, the Roman historian, says that 580,000 Jewish soldiers fell by the sword alone, in addition to those who fell by fire and famine.

6. England Expelled All of its Jewish Population

On July 18, 1290, the ninth of Av, the ruthless English king Edward I ordered the expulsion of all Jews from the nation. It would be almost four centuries before any Jews were legally allowed to live once more in the land.

7. Spain Expelled All of its Extensive Jewish Population

On August 2, 1492, the ninth of Av, the Spanish government ordered the expulsion of 800,000 Jews. This event marked a watershed in the rise of the Spanish Empire, and from this point the empire's fortunes began to decrease, possibly in fulfillment of God's promise to Abraham that "I will bless them that bless thee, and curse him that curseth thee" (Genesis 12:3). The rise and fall of many nations and empires can be traced to this prophecy and God's intervention in history.

It is interesting to note that this ninth of Av was the very same day that Christopher Columbus set sail from Spain to discover North America. This pivotal event was of tremendous importance to Jewish people, because North America ultimately provided the safest place of refuge for the Jews since they were expelled from the Holy Land. When the new nation of Israel was reborn on May 15, 1948, the United States of America became Israel's strongest protector and supporter. It is worthwhile to note that some historians suggest there is some evidence that Christopher Columbus might have been of Jewish ancestry, and that the ninth of Av 1492 was therefore an appropriate day for him to sail from Spain.

8. Russia Mobilized for World War One and Unleashed Persecutions Against the Jews

On the ninth of Av, in August 1914, as the Jews fasted and mourned, World War One was declared. As Russia mobilized its great armies, anti-Semitic persecution and severe attacks against the Jews were unleashed in eastern Russia. As a result of this persecution, many Jews were forced to immigrate to the Holy Land. These Russian and Eastern European Jewish immigrants joined the native-born Jews, the "Sabras," in building the agricultural settlements and infrastructure of the embryonic state. This immigration helped set the stage for the dramatic events of the creation of Israel in May 15, 1948.

The Remarkable Odds Against These Eight Disasters Occurring on One Day by Chance

As mentioned earlier, the phenomenon of eight major historical disasters affecting a single nation over thirty-five centuries all occurring on the same anniversary day is totally unprecedented in human history. I can assure you that I have searched, without success, for the last thirty-five years for any such pattern of historical anniversaries or "coincidences" in the history of any nation other than Israel, God's Chosen People.

In fact, I would suggest that you consider the virtual

impossibility that these eight historical tragedies could have occurred by random chance rather than by God's foreknowledge and sovereign control. Consider that there are 365 days in a year. Therefore, the chance that a second significant historical tragedy could occur by random chance alone on the very same anniversary date of a previous tragedy, say, the ninth day of Av (August), is:

$$1 \times 365, \text{ or one chance in } 365.$$

The odds against a third similar historical event occurring to the same nation on the exact same day, the ninth day of Av, is:

$$1 \times 365 \times 365 = \text{one chance in } 133,225$$

Therefore, the odds against even three of these national disasters occurring by accidental chance alone on the ninth day of Av is only one in 133,225.

The odds that all eight historical events would occur by random chance alone on the ninth day of Av, rather than by God's providential design, is equal to:

$$1 \times 365 \times 365 \times 365 \times 365 \times 365 \times 365 \times 365 \times 365 =$$
Only one chance in 863,078,009,300,000,000

It is important to note that the above probability analysis regarding these eight historical anniversary events that occurred on the ninth day of Av demonstrates that it is impossible unless God was in control of these historical events. No rational person could conclude that these key historical events in the life of Israel have happened by chance alone. The only rational explanation for this phenomenon is that God has His hand upon the Jewish people and the nation of Israel. Finally, this provides compelling evidence that the Bible, which reveals these staggering, historically verified events, is truly the inspired Word of God.

Notes

1. Grant R. Jeffrey, *Armageddon – Appointment with Destiny* (Toronto: Frontier Research Publications Inc., 1997).

14

The Witch of Endor

One of the stranger mysteries in the Bible is the curious account of King Saul of Israel visiting the witch of Endor and requiring her to call up the spirit of the departed prophet Samuel to give him desperately needed advice regarding the forthcoming battle with the Philistines. The law of God clearly prohibited witchcraft and any attempt at communication with the spirits of the dead. "Regard not them that have familiar spirits, neither seek after wizards, to be defiled by them: I am the Lord your God" (Leviticus 19:31). The Lord had clearly condemned anyone who would consult with spirits. "And the soul that turneth after such as have familiar spirits, and after wizards, to go a whoring after them, I will even set my face against that soul, and will cut him off from among his people" (Leviticus 20:6).

King Saul had relied throughout his reign upon the valued advice of the prophet Samuel and now felt abandoned by God and His prophet Samuel since the death of the man of God. Despite the fact that God had clearly outlawed witchcraft and dealing with spirits of the dead, the king in desperation sought out a witch to obtain supernatural direction in his greatest crisis: "And when Saul enquired of the Lord, the Lord answered him not, neither by dreams, nor by Urim [breastplate of High Priest], nor by prophets. Then said Saul unto his servants, Seek me a woman that hath a familiar spirit, that I may go to her, and enquire of her. And his servants said to him, Behold, there is a woman that hath a familiar spirit at Endor" (1 Samuel 28:6–7).

King Saul disguised himself and secretly visited the witch of Endor, demanding that she call up the spirit of the dead prophet of God. After securing his promise that he would not entrap her in violation of the law against witchcraft, the witch reluctantly called up the spirit of Samuel. When the apparition appeared, Saul asked her what he looked like, and he recognized that it was Samuel's spirit:

> And Samuel said to Saul, Why hast thou disquieted me, to bring me up? And Saul answered, I am sore distressed; for the Philistines make war against me, and God is departed from me, and answereth me no more, neither by prophets, nor by dreams: therefore I have called thee, that thou mayest make known unto me what I shall do. Then said Samuel, Wherefore then dost thou ask of me, seeing the Lord is departed from thee, and is become thine enemy? And the Lord hath done to him, as he spake by me: for the Lord hath rent the kingdom out of thine hand, and given it to thy neighbour, even to David: Because thou obeyedst not the voice of the Lord, nor executedst his fierce wrath upon Amalek, therefore hath the Lord done this thing unto thee this day. (1 Samuel 28:15–18)

Unfortunately for King Saul, the word of the departed prophet's apparition was the declaration of the implacable judgment of God that his crown, his life, and his family were forfeit because of his repeated disobedience against the command of God.

The mystery is this: Was the spiritual apparition a real presence of the true departed spirit of Samuel, or was it just a false representation by a demon? Some scholars have suggested that this appearance must have been a demonic apparition called forth by the witch of Endor that brought the spirit of Samuel back from the dead. However, Hebrews 9:27 assures us that death is final: "It is appointed unto men once to die, but after this the judgment." The second possibility is that the witch used spiritualistic trickery (including ventriloquism) to impersonate the spirit of the prophet Samuel. However, the Bible records that Samuel's spirit appeared and declared a true prophecy to Saul.

Therefore, I believe we should conclude that a third possibility is the truth. This mysterious event was a unique and special miracle of God to bring Samuel's spirit forth from Hades, the waiting place known as Abraham's Bosom, to proclaim the Lord's prophecy about the coming judgment upon King Saul's reign and family. The fact that the witch herself was badly frightened argues that this was a real presence of the departed spirit of Samuel that was far beyond her limited powers and experience. The ability to genuinely call up a true spirit of a departed person from Hades belongs solely to God, not to some witch. The very unusual nature of the prophetic revelation appearing in the house of a witch simply parallels other unusual occurrences throughout which God has displayed His supernatural power, such as the ass of the pagan prophet Balaam recorded in Numbers 22.

The fact that the spirit of Samuel pronounced a genuine prophecy of God regarding the approaching doom of King Saul and his family that was soon fulfilled also argues in favor of this spiritual appearance being genuine.

This unique appearance of a departed spirit under God's special supernatural power provides no encouragement or warrant for the New Age spiritualism practices of séances, channeling, or other attempts to derive information or communication from the dead. The Scriptures clearly and repeatedly forbid spiritualistic practices of any kind. "There shall not be found among you any one that maketh his son or his daughter to pass through the fire, or that useth divination, or an observer of times, or an enchanter, or a witch, or a charmer, or a consulter with familiar spirits, or a wizard, or a necromancer. For all that do these things are an abomination unto the Lord: and because of these abominations the Lord thy God doth drive them out from before thee" (Deuteronomy 18:10–12).

15

The Ezekiel Tablets

In a small locked room in Jerusalem lies a mystery and a treasure that is of tremendous archeological and spiritual importance to the nation of Israel and to all those who love the Bible. For years I had heard curious rumors about an unprecedented Israeli discovery of an entire book of the Bible that was inscribed on ancient marble tablets. In my decades of study of biblical archeology, I have never encountered another example of even a small book of the Bible being engraved on stone. Furthermore, this text of the book of Ezekiel carved on these sixty-six extraordinary marble and basalt tablets was created by the artist in bas-relief. This is a laborious and painstaking method of stone carving in which the background stone is carefully removed, leaving the thousands of letters in bold relief approximately a quarter-inch higher than the marble background. It would take a least one hundred times the effort and time to construct this long text of Ezekiel in bas-relief than to use the normal engraving method. If the craftsman made one error in a letter, then the entire stone tablet would have to be replaced.

During a trip to Israel twelve years ago, I tracked down the location of this unusual find with great difficulty. After many hours of following false leads and rumors throughout Jerusalem, my wife Kaye and I finally approached a small obscure house and observed a remarkable garden wall decorated with a magnificent mosaic image of a lion. The house had a small sign identifying it as Yad Ben Zvi (House of Ben Zvi). It housed the Ben Zvi Institute, an institution that studied the history of the Jews during their many centuries of exile from their Promised Land. When I asked four different Israeli employees about the marble tablets, each told us that what we were seeking did not exist. They suggested that we were misinformed and must be looking for something else, perhaps the ancient "Tomb of Jason," located several blocks away.

However, as we wandered in the grounds we came to a locked door that led to an adjoining room of the Ben Zvi Institute. I knew that my information was correct. It took several days to find someone who had the authority and willingness to allow us to examine this hidden treasure. Through the good offices of an Israeli friend named Dan Setton, a documentary film producer who knew the people in charge of the Ben Zvi Institute as a result of a previous film documentary, we were finally given the privilege of examining and photographing these tablets in detail. This section includes several photographs of these spectacular Ezekiel Tablets, revealing their remarkable features.

The Tomb of Ezekiel the prophet in Kafr Al-Kafil, on the Euphrates River in Iraq.

This discovery could ultimately change our understanding of the transmission of biblical texts throughout the centuries. The Israelis who have these treasured tablets call them the Eze-kiel Tablets. There are sixty-six stone tablets, mostly in marble, several in black basalt, that contain over two-thirds of the text of the Book of Ezekiel, inscribed in bas-relief. The prophet Ezekiel foretold events of profound importance to modern Israel that will occur as the time for the coming of the Messiah draws near. The message of the Exile and their return to the Promised Land, of the coming war of Gog and Magog, of the rebuilding of the Temple when the Messiah and the *Shekinah* glory of God return to Israel are imprinted on these sacred tablets.

The marble tablets are located in a small museum in the house of the late Ben Zvi, the second president of Israel, a very religious career diplomat and dedicated amateur archeologist. He became president in November 1952, following the death of Israel's first president, Chaim Wiezmann. President Ben Zvi lived in a very simple house that has now been transformed into a religious institute and a museum. The Institute is called Yad Ben Zvi, dedicated to his memory and to studying the history of the Jewish experience during thousands of years of exile from Israel. Within its walls are study halls and a publishing house that deals with Jewish history. The curator of the small adjoin-ing museum housing the Ezekiel Tablets is Yehuda Oppenheim, a friend of the late president. Research is continuing regarding the origin and meaning of these unique stones, as there is still much to be learned regarding the reason for their creation and the time of their inscription.

During World War II, a Jewish man named David Cohen was living in Syria, where he met a French woman who described to him some unusual Hebrew inscribed stone tablets she had in her possession. She was trying to return to France, and the tablets were much too heavy to transport in wartime conditions. She was concerned about what might happen to them if she left them behind while the war continued. She was hoping that someone would help her place the tablets in the hands of appropriate scholars.

One day she traveled to British-occupied Jerusalem and

spoke with her priest about the inscribed stones. He encouraged her to find a way to return them to the Holy Land, because he believed that the stones with the inscribed Hebrew script belonged to the Jewish people. The woman stayed in Syria until World War II ended and kept the tablets with her. Later, during Israel's War of Independence in 1948, she met David Cohen again and was finally convinced to do something with the tablets. The two of them arranged to transfer the tablets from Damascus to Beirut and from there to the northern border of Israel, where they were privately stored in Lebanon for safekeeping for several years during those uncertain times. When Ben Zvi became Israel's president in 1952, Cohen transferred the tablets to Ben Zvi's home in Jerusalem, where they were stored in a strong room without any serious scholarly examination. The extraordinary political and military crisis of the day prevented President Ben Zvi from devoting the time he wished to resolve the puzzle of the origin of these Ezekiel Tablets.

The French woman had told Cohen that her father-in-law, a French doctor and amateur archeologist, received the marble tablets as payment for medical services he had provided to members of an Arab tribe while in the eastern Syrian Desert early in the 1900s. Occasionally these Bedouin Arabs paid him with archeological materials instead of money. The Arab tribesmen told him that they had taken these tablets from the ancient tomb of the prophet Ezekiel, near the Euphrates River. This tomb of Ezekiel is located sixty miles south of Baghdad, Iraq, in the small Arab village of Kaffeil Arhut. Like the cave tombs in Hebron, Israel, the tomb has multiple caves with upper and lower levels. These stones were supposedly transported from Ezekiel's tomb to Syria, where they were ultimately given to the doctor-archeologist. When the tablets finally found a home in the small museum in Jerusalem, a large donation was provided by an interested Jewish citizen, which enabled the museum to build a glassed exhibit to properly display these tablets to a few scholars and interested rabbis.

One reason this is such an important archeological find is the unique nature of the tablets: a complete biblical text on marble tablets, not on scrolls of parchment or leather. A brief mention of the tablets appeared in an unnamed professional archeological journal many years ago, but there were few details regarding their location. Aside from a small group of individuals, including my friend and a respected prophecy teacher Dr. David Lewis, very few people have examined these stones. Several knowledgeable archeologists and rabbis in Israel initially told me it was impossible that such an archeological treasure could exist in Israel without their knowing of it. They were convinced only when they examined my photographs and then contacted the Ben Zvi Institute authorities for confirmation.

The small number of scholars who have seen the Ezekiel Tablets is divided as to initial conclusions about the origin of the tablets. While a few Israeli scholars believe that the inscription may actually date back to the time of Ezekiel; the majority favor the view that the tablets were created at some point during the Middle Ages. However, both groups believe that these unique biblical stone tablets are extraordinary in their significance to Bible textual scholarship and are deserving of further study.

Most of the Israeli and North American scholars who have examined these stones believe that the available evidence indicates they were created approximately one thousand years ago. The basic reason for their conclusion is textual, related to the shape of the raised Hebrew letters. The study of writing, known as orthography, suggests that the beautifully decorative style of the chiseled letters on the tablets follows the square Aramaic form that became increasingly common several centuries after the destruction of Jerusalem in A.D. 70. These scholars also point to large areas of "clean writing" in the inscriptions which suggests a more recent dating. Every one of the twenty-two Hebrew letters is present on the tablets, including several examples of "final Memes" ending sentences that tend to indicate a more recent date. This style of writing appears to these scholars to be much later than the sixth century B.C., when the prophet Ezekiel lived in Babylon. If they are correct, some Jewish master craftsman may have created the tablets for a wealthy Jewish patron or synagogue at some point during the Middle Ages. However, a Hebrew script from Egypt, which is clearly dated from the sixth century B.C., was discovered recently that contains letters almost identical to the Ezekiel Tablet letters. The importance of this development is that it suggests the clear possibility that these marble tablets do in fact date back to the centuries long before the time of Christ.

However, several Israeli scholars connected with the Ben Zvi Institute museum suggest that these marble tablets may actually be a copy of the original text of the book of Ezekiel placed for safekeeping in the prophet's tomb, either created by the prophet himself or, more probably, by his pupils following his death. There is an ancient tradition in the Jewish *Talmud* that states the original book of Ezekiel was buried in the prophet's tomb and left there to be revealed in the last days. These scholars claim this would help to explain why such a biblical textual treasure was hidden and remained unknown for so many centuries. They also point to several examples of "defective writing" in these inscriptions, which may suggest an early date several centuries before the birth of Christ.

The Hebrew letters are inscribed on the marble tablets in bas-relief. This would take a hundred times more effort and expert craftsmanship than engraving or chiseling into the stone in the normal manner. Biblical archeologists in Chicago have told me there is no known example of any other extensive biblical text

The Ezekiel Tablets. The collection contains 66 marble tablets (some are basalt). Two-thirds of the text of the book of Ezekiel are present.

inscribed in bas-relief on stone. Nor is there any known book of the Bible inscribed on stone, even with the normal chiseled engraving method. Israeli scholars who support an earlier date, back to the time of Ezekiel, suggest that one of the possible reasons Ezekiel or his students chose to create the tablets in bas-relief is that it would prevent any future tampering with the sacred text. Not a single letter, "jot or tittle," can be added to such a bas-relief inscription without its being immediately detected.

I have discovered that several other extensive non-biblical inscriptions were carved in bas-relief on stone during the time of Ezekiel. These inscriptions were found in Lebanon high up on the rock cliffs of Wadi Brissa in the 1800s. They were created by the Babylonian king Nebuchadnezzar's craftsmen on an expedition to conquer Lebanon in 588 B.C. The Babylonian army took enormous numbers of beautiful cedars back to his capital to use in his palaces, and in this bas-relief inscription, the king declares his exploits and prays to his god, "O Merodach, my lord, my champion. . . . At thy exalted word, which changes not, may my wood cutting prosper. May the work of my hands come to completion."[1] This inscription provides historical confirmation about King Nebuchadnezzar's activities as described

Close-up revealing the bas relief script. The letters display an ornate decorative style, using the square Aramaic script.

in the Book of Daniel. It also reveals that such labor-intensive bas-relief stone inscriptions were used at the precise time the prophet Ezekiel was a captive in Babylon.

Israeli scholars could not determine how ancient craftsmen could produce the entire book of Ezekiel by this unusually difficult procedure of bas relief marble stone carving. If the artisan made only one mistake, he would have had to destroy an entire tablet. The amount of work involved in producing these sixty-six stones in bas-relief script is almost unimaginable, especially if the purpose was purely decorative. The cost and time involved would be prohibitive, even for a wealthy patron. If such an incredible treasure is only one thousand years old and existed in some wealthy Jewish mansion or synagogue for hundreds of years, why is there no reference to or legend about such wonderful, priceless objects?

The existing tablets contain over two-thirds of the text of the book of Ezekiel. Less than one-third is missing, and the missing tablets are distributed randomly throughout the different chapters of Ezekiel's text. There is some indication from sources I have interviewed that missing tablets may be in the hands of private collectors, or that they might have been secretly taken to France. The scholars at the museum are anxious to recover the missing tablets, or at least acquire photos or copies from them for further research.

There is another curious feature regarding the tablets. While most of the sixty-six tablets are of marble, some of the text is inscribed on black basalt. If the purpose of creating the tablets was purely artistic for a wealthy patron or synagogue, why wouldn't the craftsman use marble throughout? Anyone with enough money and the expert craftsmen to produce most of the work on marble stones, which is excellent for long-term preservation, would not normally switch to black basalt for the few remaining pieces of text. They do not match; black basalt is an inferior stone of far less value and does not last nearly as long.

However, some Israeli scholars suggest that if the Jewish slaves living during the Babylonian Captivity (606–53 B.C.) inscribed these tablets, it is possible that they could not get enough marble to complete the whole text and had to use the less expensive but widely available black basalt. Marble cannot be found in Babylon; it was usually imported at great cost. Normally, in such archeological finds where different materials are found in 10 percent or so of the writing, some damage has occurred that necessitated repairs. If the craftsmen could not match the original stone exactly, they would usually choose a better grade of stone. For example, they might upgrade from black basalt to a richer, longer-lasting marble for the replacement pieces. However, that is not the case with these Ezekiel Tablets. The craftsmen obviously used marble throughout the project until they were forced at some point to use inferior basalt stone for a few replacement tablets in scattered areas of the text. If they created these tablets during a period of slavery, such as the Babylonian Captivity, we can easily imagine a situation in which they ran out of marble, found it impossible to acquire any more, and had to switch to basalt to complete the job. Obviously, the bas-relief technique would easily lead to errors, so that damage to the raised letters required the tablet to be replaced. One area that must still be explored is the origin of the marble: since every vein of marble is quite distinct, like a fingerprint, it is possible that a geological line of inquiry will enable researcher to determine where and when these tablets were first created.

The main factor that convinces most scholars the tablets were created long after Ezekiel's time is the style of Hebrew letters. During the time Ezekiel lived, the monarchical Hebrew script was the common style of writing. However, these tablets were written in the Hebrew-Aramaic square script developed in later centuries. Some Israeli scholars suggest that the original Hebrew letters began to change around the fifth or sixth century B.C. because of a decision by the great Hebrew leaders, Ezra and Nehemiah. At that time, scholars claim a new form was given to the Hebrew letters, which we now call the square Aramaic script. The two forms are similar, but definitely differ in their details. As an example of this major evolution in the style of letters, a Hebrew inscription from the Second Temple period is almost unreadable to a modern Israeli who reads a Hebrew newspaper.

The Israeli scholars who support the earlier dating suggest that Ezra and Nehemiah introduced the new Aramaic style Hebrew script only seventy years after Ezekiel. Otherwise, changes would not have been officially accepted by the population or by the Great Sanhedrin (the Jewish court of religious law). These scholars claim that if this square Aramaic script was first introduced by the prophet Ezekiel on the marble tablets as the inspired Word of God, this would explain why Ezra and Nehemiah would officially command its legitimacy seventy years later, around 520 B.C.

Changes in forms or shapes of letters in a language usually evolve over hundreds of years and proceed at different paces in different nations. For example, in my own library are English books written from 1650 onwards. The shapes and uses of the letters change from book to book. At one point the letter "f" was used for an "s" in one country, while another country had already switched to the new "s". Some scholars report that the square Aramaic Hebrew script was introduced gradually from the eighth century B.C. until its universal adoption in the second century following Christ. However, I have recently learned of a Hebrew script that appears to date from the sixth century B.C. in Egypt with letters almost identical to those in the Ezekiel Tablets.

During a fascinating discussion with the scholars at the institute about the possibility that the Ezekiel Tablets may date back to the prophet's exile in Babylon, someone asked about their official position on the dating and origin of the tablets. In light of their obvious enthusiasm, their somewhat surprising answer was: "Our position is that the tablets are only one thousand years old." When pressed to explain why they took this position, they allegedly admitted their real reason: "If the stones are [officially] only one thousand years old, our [Ben Zvi] institute can keep them. If they are proven to truly date back to the period of Ezekiel, then the government would take them and build their own museum to house them, like the Dead Sea Scrolls. We would then lose the Ezekiel Tablets. So our position is that they are only one thousand years old."

Competent Hebrew scholars have privately stated that these tablets are one of the most interesting textual finds in the history of archeology. If they were ever proven to date back to the period before Christ, the Ezekiel Tablets would be almost as important a textual find as the precious Dead Sea Scrolls that transformed the world of biblical textual scholarship. Whether the ultimate conclusion is that the tablets are a thousand years old or much older, dating back 2600 years to the time of the prophet Ezekiel, this archeological discovery will have a profound effect upon our understanding of the creation and transmission of biblical texts through the centuries.

The Jewish commentary on the Law, the *Talmud (Megilla,* 26b), records the ancient Jewish custom of burying the original manuscripts within the tomb of their sages and scholars.[2] The *Talmud* states that the tomb of Ezekiel near Babylon is not far from the tomb of Baruch, the scribe who assisted the prophet Jeremiah by recording his inspired biblical prophecies. The Bible does not indicate that Baruch ever traveled to Babylon or that he was buried there. However, it is possible that Baruch traveled there in his later life to visit the large Jewish community living in captivity in Babylon some six hundred miles from Jerusalem. The first group of Persians who attempted to break into Ezekiel's tomb was killed supernaturally, according to the legends of the *Talmud*.

There is another ancient legend about a Persian prince who asked the Jews to fast and pray in an attempt to discover the correct way to accomplish his purpose. After many days of fasting, the Jewish leaders suggested that they first attempt to open the tomb of the scribe Baruch and then try to enter the tomb of the prophet Ezekiel. Once they successfully entered the tomb of Ezekiel, they were surprised to discover the remains of a body lying on marble tablets. This reference to marble tablets within the tomb of Ezekiel in an ancient Jewish text is intriguing. Could these marble tablets in the legend be the same tablets that the Bedouin Arabs took from the tomb of Ezekiel more than a thousand years later? While this account does not prove that the Ezekiel Tablets came from the ancient tomb of the prophet, it certainly provides some intriguing evidence in favor of that conclusion.

Another fascinating historical footnote is connected to the tomb of Ezekiel. In Louis Ginzberg's famous book, *Legends of the Jews*, he describes an ancient tradition of the Jews of Babylon, recording an attempt that was made by robbers to break into the tomb of the prophet "to take some books from the grave of

Ezekiel." It is interesting to note that the legend reveals that the attempt to steal the "books" was unsuccessful.[3] The word translated "books" could refer only to either scrolls or stone tablets, since the ancient Jews did not possess bound books with pages at that time. This ancient Jewish reference lends support to the Arab account that they actually took these marble tablets from Ezekiel's tomb during the early 1900s.

The Lost Treasures of King Solomon's Temple

One of the questions that has perplexed both rabbis and archeologists is the mystery of the hidden location of the vast amount of gold and silver treasures from Solomon's Temple that went missing at that time. The ancient Jewish commentaries reveal that the interior walls of the Temple were covered with great quantities of precious gold, and that enormous numbers of gold vessels, silver objects, and costly jewels filled the Temple treasury. When the Babylonian army under King Nebuchadnezzar invaded Judah (587 B.C.) and besieged Jerusalem, the prophet Jeremiah repeatedly warned the Jewish King Zedekiah and his nobles that God's judgment was about the fall upon that wicked generation which had ignored years of divine warnings to Israel. During the brutal months of siege, the Temple priests charged with guarding the sacred treasures of the sanctuary certainly had time to plan and carry out a mission to safeguard these precious Temple objects.

When King Solomon built the Temple, he followed an exact blueprint provided by God to his father King David. In addition to the surface buildings of the magnificent Temple, there were numerous subterranean cisterns, secret repositories, and many hidden escape tunnels carved out of the soft limestone rock that formed Mount Moriah upon which the vast Temple structures were constructed. My wife Kaye and I have personally spent many hours exploring and photographing these ancient tunnels and rooms hidden beneath the Temple Mount, including Solomon's Stables (see my documentary video *Archeological Discoveries: Exploring Beneath the Temple Mount*, Order Form, end of book).

The Jewish historian Flavius Josephus referred to a two-thousand-year-old escape tunnel constructed by King Herod that led from the Tower of Antonia to the Eastern Gate to allow the king to escape his enemies in the event of an attack.[4] Several of my Israeli friends also recently discovered a remarkable escape tunnel carved out of the limestone rock that led from the ancient Temple eleven miles to the east beneath Wadi Kelt, through the Judean Desert toward Jericho, where King Herod had his summer palace. The many years of brutal labor that would have been required to carve out such a long escape tunnel through the limestone is extraordinary.

While the Bible records that the Babylonian army stole many of the treasures of the Temple and took them back to Babylon, there are strong indications that the Ark of the Covenant, as well as many other sacred vessels was not among these looted treasures captured by Nebuchadnezzar's pagan army. If the Temple priests were successful in hiding the most important of the Temple treasures, the questions that arise are these: Where did they hide these important treasures? Are they still hidden in secret locations awaiting the arrival of the messianic era when they will be needed once more by the Jewish priests to resume the Temple worship as described in the Bible's prophecies?

About ten years ago, after I began my successful search to verify the curious story about the lost Ezekiel Tablets, I met an Israeli, Yehuda Oppenheim, who was involved with the museum that possesses the mysterious marble tablets. Oppenheim told me that he had been searching for several years to find an article in a decades-old archeological journal that someone had told him contained a definite reference to the elusive tablets in a brief paragraph and photo. Unfortunately, despite years of searching, Yehuda Oppenheim could not find the journal partly because his source could not remember the name of the journal, and only knew that it was a foreign-language publication.

Fortunately, during a subsequent visit to the Hebrew University library in Jerusalem, I had an opportunity to examine their extensive collection of archeological journals dealing with the Middle East that goes back one hundred and fifty years. After several hours of research in their vast library, I finally tracked down a reference to an article about the Copper Scroll in a volume within an enormous group of documents and volumes covering an entire wall of their library. In the 1959 issue of the scientific journal *Revue Biblique* I found an article by archeologist Dr. J. Milik (one of the major Dead Sea Scroll scholars) on the Copper Scroll, which described the hidden location of sixty-four of the treasures from the Second Temple (described in chapter 16 of this book).[5] To my great surprise, when I opened the French text dealing with the Copper Scroll, near the end of Milik's article I found a photo of one of the missing marble tablets, with a partial description of the Hebrew text and how Milik had found the marble tablets in Lebanon. His friend, Dr. Jean Starcky, another famous Dead Sea Scroll scholar, took the photo. Strangely, the photo of the marble tablet and the translated text were not listed in either the subject index or the article titles of *Revue Biblique,* which made it difficult for anyone to find it. This vital information about the marble tablets was simply buried in an unrelated article about the Copper Scroll. Despite years of searching, Oppenheim and his other researchers could not find the obscure reference to these marble tablets because, as a side issue to the article, it was not indexed. The only connection in Milik's article between the Copper Scroll, which deals with the Second Temple, and the Ezekiel Tablets, which include the book of Ezekiel and the final two tablets describing King Solomon's Temple treasures, is that both of these ancient non-biblical writings contain secret information about where the treasures of the two Jewish Temples were hidden from the two separate invading pagan armies.

Milik's article also contained the long-sought-after paragraph with the Hebrew text and a photo of one of the two (still missing) marble tablets. Milik related the fact that these marble tablets were photographed in the late 1940s in a basement in Beirut, Lebanon. In addition to recording that these remarkable marble tablets contained the entire text of Ezekiel carved in bas-relief, the article described the text found on two additional marble tablets that contained an extraordinary account of the secret burial of the long-lost treasures from King Solomon's Temple before they could be looted by the King Nebuchadnezzar's army when the Temple was destroyed in 587 B.C.

Now that I had located the mysterious photo, I was able to obtain a translation of the ancient Hebrew text. The photo revealed a marble tablet with an unusual text in ancient Hebrew script carved in bas-relief—identical to the textual style found in the other Ezekiel Tablets. However, the mysterious text in the photo did not contain the text of the book of Ezekiel. Rather, it contained a history of the hiding of the lost treasures of Solomon's Temple and their secret locations near Mount Carmel.

The article (in French) in *Revue Biblique* states:

> The copper scroll originating in Cave 3 of Qumran has a catalog of treasures hidden in the underground of Palestine. . . . Another writing most interesting because it relates in detail the treasures of the Temple of Jerusalem hidden about the time of the destruction by the Babylonians [in 587 B.C.]. It was printed in 1853 by A. Jellinek in Bet-ha-Midrash II, Leipzig, pages 26 and 85–91 (which the author of this article did not find available). A duplicate of this *Treatise of the Sacred Vessels* is to be read on the "Plates (tablets) of Beirut."

> A good number of years ago he found in a house in Beirut several marble slabs engraved with letters in relief. It seems they were destined for a synagogue of Syria or Lebanon. They contained the entire text of Ezekiel, but on the two last slabs were found inscribed the history of a treasure of Mount Carmel and the description of the sacred hiding places. . . these slabs are worth further study to determine the date of the writing.[6]

This fascinating article reveals that Milik knew the last two marble tablets regarding the treasures of Solomon's Temple were part of the Ezekiel Tablets, containing the complete text of the book of Ezekiel. At some point in the late 1940s, Milik had seen the Ezekiel Tablets in Beirut, Lebanon, and felt they were certainly worthy of further study by qualified scholars. Now after all these years, they have found a permanent home in Jerusalem.

Hopefully, scholars from around the world will now be able to complete the essential research to determine the true source and dating of these mysterious tablets. But for now, the mystery of the Ezekiel Tablets and their clues regarding the location of the fabled lost treasures of King Solomon's golden Temple remains unsolved.

Notes

1. Stephen Langdon, *Building Inscriptions of the New Babylonian Empire* (Paris:, 1905) 151.
2. Talmud, *Megilla*, 26b.
3. Louis Ginzberg, *Legends of the Jews,* Vol. IV (Philadelphia: The Jewish Publication 4. Society of America, 1968). 324–326.
4. Flavius Josephus, *Antiquities of the Jews.*
5. J. Milik, "Copper Scroll" *Revue Biblique,* 1959.
6. J. Milik, "Copper Scroll" *Revue Biblique,* 1959.

16

The Lost Treasures
of the Temple

One of the most interesting mysteries in Bible archeology revolves around what happened to the lost treasures from the Second Temple. During the final months of the Roman army's long siege of the sacred Temple (A.D. 70), the armed members of two Jewish sects, the Essenes and the Zealots, were in total control of the holy Sanctuary. There are numerous Jewish traditions and legends that some of the precious treasures of the Temple were carefully hidden away from the avarice of the Roman army, who ultimately looted the sacred treasury. The discovery by archeologists of many secret subterranean tunnels deep beneath the surface of the Temple Mount reveals that the priests and Temple guards had ample means of hiding these treasures and escaping the siege with various movable objects.

When the Dead Sea Scrolls were discovered in a cave at Qumran by an Arab boy in 1947, the attention of the world was focused upon these remarkable two-thousand-year-old manuscripts, which included ancient copies of virtually every one of the books of the Old Testament. These manuscripts threw new light on the religious beliefs and events that occurred in the century when Christianity was created and the Jewish Temple was destroyed. In March 1953, another curious scroll was discovered in Cave number 3 Q 15, only a mile north of the ruins of the ancient village of Qumran on the west side of the Dead Sea. Out of thousands of manuscript fragments discovered in the Dead Sea Caves, all of them were written on parchment or leather, save this one. The scroll found in Cave 3 Q 15 was composed of three copper sheets riveted together to form a single sheet eight feet long and one foot wide. This manuscript became known as the Copper Scroll.

The author had painstakingly engraved Hebrew letters into the copper sheet with several carved chisels. The metal had deteriorated over two thousand years to the point that the archeologists were unable to easily unroll the scroll to read it. But after several years of careful work, the brittle metal scroll was unraveled and translated. Using a jeweler's saw, they finally cut the tightly rolled scroll sideways to allow access to the writing. The Copper Scroll revealed a detailed list of sixty-four secret locations where the priests had carefully hidden the gold and silver treasures from the Temple. The amount and value of the buried Temple treasure listed in the scroll was breathtaking, including a number of sacred Temple vessels, manuscripts, and the breastplate of the high priest.

A number of Dead Sea Scroll archeologists, led by Professor J. T. Milik, concluded that this list was only a mythological buried-treasure tale.[1] The main reason many scholars have rejected the possibility that the Copper Scroll might actually refer to real Temple treasures has to do with the enormous size of the treasure described, which amounted to some 3,282 talents of gold and 1,280 talents of silver. Since a talent is equivalent to almost a hundred pounds of metal, the total of over 4,500 talents amounted to 7,200,000 ounces of precious metal, and at today's prices for gold and silver would have a value exceeding $650 million (U.S.). Naturally, many scholars concluded that the size of the treasure proved that the list must be a legend or imaginary. However, in defense of the possibility that the Copper Scroll list is genuine, we should remember that the Temple contained vast amounts of the wealth of the Jewish nation, in addition to its precious worship vessels of gold and silver.

The Jewish historian Flavius Josephus in his *Antiquities of the Jews* states that when General Pompey captured Jerusalem in 63 B.C. he demanded and received an immediate tribute to Rome of "more than 10,000 talents" from the Temple treasury in Jerusalem.[2] The Temple treasury contained an enormous quantity of sacred Temple treasures, but it also acted as a central bank for the nation and a well-guarded repository bank for wealthy individuals and the government.

Could the Copper Scroll contain information revealing the actual location of buried objects from the Temple? There were over 4,000 members of the Essene sect during the first century. In addition to Temple treasures, the hidden amounts could also have contained the accumulated wealth of the Essenes themselves, at that time a two-hundred-year-old religious community at Qumran and Jerusalem. The German archeologist Dr. Bargil Pixner discovered evidence of the Essenes' community on Mount Zion in Jerusalem, including the Essene Gate,[3] and he has shared a great deal of valuable information with me regarding his archeological research on the Essenes and the Copper Scroll.[4] Over two centuries they could have accumulated a huge treasury, because each member turned over his wealth to the group when he first joined.

The list of treasures in the Copper Scroll is a very basic accounting of objects. There is no embellishment of details as you would expect to find if the list were imaginary. Many of the sixty-four hidden locations were in caves and cisterns surrounding Wadi Ha Kippah, the wadi (valley) in which the majority of the Dead Sea Scrolls were found in Cave 4 close by the ruined village of Qumran. This ancient valley has been identified as the valley of Qumran, based on ancient maps and exact references to a series of toponyms. These geographically detailed descriptions may enable future investigators to determine the location of several of the listed hiding places.

There are three major areas described in the Copper Scroll as locations of the hidden treasures: Qumran, Jerusalem, and the Yarmuk River area east of the Jordan River in present-day Jordan. These three locations were known to be major centers of Essene settlement and activity.

As an example, I will give Pixner's translation of the description for site 54 in the Copper Scroll: "Close by (BTKN ' SLM) on the treading place (BHBSH) at the top of the rock facing west against the garden of Sadok, under the great stone slab of the water outlet: untouchable (anathema!) (HRM)."

This particular item is definitely a sacred object from the Temple itself. A special curse was proclaimed against any unauthorized person disturbing its resting place. Many details of the descriptions are subject to interpretation. One of the problems is that a great deal of wind and occasional water erosion has transformed the smaller geographical features of the Qumran area.

The list was composed during the siege of the Temple by a member of the Essenes in A.D. 68 and buried in Cave 3, were it lay undisturbed for nineteen centuries until its discovery in 1952. Professor R. de Vaux, one of the major Dead Sea Scroll scholars, wrote, "None of the works could have been composed, and none of the manuscripts either written, copied, or placed in the caves after June A.D. 68, the point at which the life of the community of Qumran was brought to an end." [5] If any of the Essene group had survived, the Copper Scroll would have been removed. The fact that the scroll was still in the cave suggests that the Roman army killed all of the Essenes. Obviously, many of the treasure sites would have been discovered accidentally by various people digging cisterns and buildings, et cetera, at different times over the centuries. However, if the Copper Scroll is genuine, several of the treasures may have escaped chance discovery. Over the next few years a group of archeologists are beginning a systematic search of the area, examining the clues to additional locations suggested by the Copper Scroll.

In April 1988, a team of archeologists began to search for one of the hidden Temple treasures listed in the Copper Scroll that was reportedly buried near Qumran. Following the geographical directions found in the scroll, the investigators discovered a cave that contained the hidden oil of anointing, lost almost two thousand years ago. In February 15, 1989, the *New York Times* reported the find.[6] One of the most important of the missing treasures of the Temple was the specially consecrated oil of anointing that was used to anoint the kings of Israel, the Ark of the Covenant, and the other Temple vessels. The oil of anointing, sometimes called the *Shemen Afarshimon* is referred to in Psalm 133. "It is like the precious ointment upon the head, that ran down upon the beard, even Aaron's beard: that went down to the skirts of his garments" (Psalms 133:2). The sacred oil was also used as the fragrance on the oblation for a sweet-smelling savor on the sacrifices.

During the Exodus, God commanded Moses to create the oil of anointing using five special ingredients.

> And thou shalt make it an oil of holy ointment, an ointment compound after the art of the apothecary: it shall be an holy anointing oil. And thou shalt anoint the tabernacle of the congregation therewith, and the ark of the testimony. . . . And thou shalt anoint Aaron and his sons, and consecrate them, that they may minister unto me in the priest's office. And thou shalt speak unto the children of Israel, saying, This shall be an holy anointing oil unto me throughout your generations. (Exodus 30:25–26, 30–31)

Using the information from the Copper Scroll, an archeological team including my friend Dr. Gary Collett, began to search Cave 11 and found a clay vessel approximately five inches high that contained oil that was solidified as a gelatin-like substance, somewhat like molasses. The clay jug containing the ancient oil had been wrapped in palm leaves. It was buried three feet deep in a pit, which assisted in its preservation from the extreme high temperatures.

When this ancient oil was analyzed, the oil proved to be composed of five special ingredients, exactly as the Bible commanded Moses to use in the creation of the oil of anointing (*Shemen HaMish'chah*) as recorded in Exodus 30. Carbon 14 radioactive dating tests indicate that this oil is almost two thousand years old, from the time of the Second Temple. The *Talmud* declares that a drop of this special oil will cause water to turn white. It is alleged that this oil found at the site turned water white. Despite the incredibly high temperature in the Dead Sea caves, the lowest and hottest place on earth, the clay flask of oil remained undisturbed over the centuries. The Israel Museum verified that the composition of this ancient oil is unlike that of any other oil their scientists have ever evaluated. Intensive testing by the Pharmaceutical Department of Hebrew University established that the oil inside the clay vessel was the ancient oil of anointing.

One of the five ingredients of this anointing oil was the rare persimmon or balsam oil, known as *afarshimon*, which was so valued by Egyptian Queen Cleopatra that she asked her lover, the Roman general Mark Anthony, to give her a grove of these balsam trees in a wadi near Jericho. In fact, there were only two groves in the whole of the Middle East where the precious *afarshimon* oil grew—the one in Jericho and another in a wadi near En Gedi on the west side of the Dead Sea.

When it was obvious that the Romans were going to destroy Jerusalem and the sacred Temple, the Jewish priests burned the two precious groves of balsam trees to keep the holy anointing oil out of the hands of the Romans. However, with the destruction of the balsam groves, it became impossible to reconstitute the ancient oil of anointing according to the command of God. Some Jewish scholars argued that this inability to create the legitimate oil of anointing due to the loss of this particular species of balsam (*afarshimon*), one of the five ingredients, would prevent the Jews from ever rebuilding the Third Temple and the resumption of Temple worship services. Without the sacred oil of anointing, it would seem to be impossible to resume the Temple worship services as prophesied in the Word of God. However, the remarkable discovery of this ancient sample of the oil of anointing provides the oil necessary for the anointing of the Temple, the sacred vessels, the Cohanim, and Messiah-King of Israel.

Jesus' name "Christ" and "Messiah" includes the prophecy that He will someday be "anointed" by sacred oil as the King of Israel. In the Greek language, Jesus' title of Messiah is "Christus" or Christ. His Hebrew title is "Moshiach" which means Messiah or Anointed One. The prophecy of Daniel 9:24

declares that the final conclusion of the Seventy Weeks' Vision of Daniel the Prophet will occur when they "anoint the most Holy." Daniel's prophecy indicates that the end of this age and the commencement of the millennial Kingdom will involve the "anointing of the most Holy." Jesus of Nazareth was never anointed as Israel's Messiah during his first Advent almost two thousand years ago. In the Gospel of John, the apostle wrote, "Then took Mary a pound of ointment of spikenard, very costly, and anointed the feet of Jesus" (John 12:3). Although the woman Mary anointed His feet with valuable perfumed oil, this act did not fulfill Daniel's prophecy.

What are the implications of this remarkable discovery of the ancient and sacred oil of anointing? I believe that the finding of the oil of anointing may well prove to be a key event in setting the stage for the fulfillment of the prophecies in the last days in connection with the rebuilding of the Temple and the Second Coming of Jesus Christ as the promised Messiah.

It is possible that Jesus will finally be anointed by the high priest with the consecrated oil of anointing as Israel's Messiah when He returns in glory to save Jerusalem, cleanse the Third Temple, and establish His Kingdom forever. It is significant that the precious oil of anointing, lost for thousands of years, should be discovered in our generation. It is now in the possession of the two chief rabbis of Israel for safekeeping. When the Lord returns to set up His kingdom, the oil of anointing may finally be used to usher in His messianic rule.

Notes

1. J. T. Milik, *Discoveries in the Judean Desert*, Vol. III (Oxford: publisher, year) 199–302.
2. Flavius Josephus, *Antiquities of the Jews*, XIV, trans. Translator name (city: publisher, year) 4, 5, 7, 8.
3. Bargil Pixner, "Unravelling the Copper Scroll Doce: A Study on the Topography of 3Q15," *Revue de Qumran* 43 (1983).
4. Bargil Pixner, "Unravelling the Copper Scroll Doce: A Study on the Topography of 3Q15," *Revue de Qumran* 43 (1983).
5. Rolland. de Vaux, *Archeology and the Dead Sea Scrolls* (Oxford: Oxford University Press, 1973) 107.
6. New York Times 15 Feb. 1989.

17

The Virgin Birth of Christ

The Bible's claim that Jesus of Nazareth was born of a virgin is one of the greatest and the most mysterious miracles recorded in the Word of God. The Lord's grace and mercy was revealed to Adam and Eve immediately following His discovery of their disobedience regarding His command to not eat of the fruit of the tree of the knowledge of good and evil. Though the immediate consequence of Adam and Eve's rebellion was their permanent expulsion from the Garden of Eden, God promised that He would ultimately send His Redeemer, who would defeat the plans of Satan and destroy his seed forever. God's promise of the coming Messiah in Genesis 3:15 is the first prophecy in the Bible regarding the Virgin Birth of "the seed of the woman," the Messiah. God's prophecy included the bruising of the Messiah's heel by the serpent (Satan) and the ultimate triumph of God when the promised seed (Jesus Christ) will finally bruise the serpent's seed (the Antichrist). In the Scripture's first prophecy we find the promise of the Virgin Birth of the Messiah in the phrase, "the seed of the woman." Throughout the Bible and in all of the texts of the ancient Middle East, a child is always called "the seed of the man," never the "seed of the woman." This verse, Genesis 3:15, clearly indicated that the promised child would not be born from a man's seed, as all other children, but would be born from "the seed of a woman." In other words, this miraculous birth would be to a virgin woman without the benefit of a human father.

The prophet Isaiah wrote, "Therefore the Lord himself shall give you a sign; Behold, a virgin shall conceive, and bear a son, and shall call his name Immanuel" (Isaiah 7:14). His name "Immanuel" means "God with us." Seven centuries before the birth of Jesus, Isaiah prophesied that a supernatural "sign" would be given to Israel when a virgin would conceive and give birth to a male child. Though some liberal critics have tried to deny the significance of Isaiah's prophecy about a virgin birth, the original word used by Isaiah is *almah*. Some scholars suggest that the word *almah*, translated as "young woman," does not precisely mean "virgin" as we use the word today. While pointing out that *almah* does not primarily and solely refer to the virginal sexual status of a girl, these scholars must also admit that the word *almah* does clearly refer to "a young unmarried girl." The definition of *almah* as "a young unmarried girl" obviously implies that the unmarried girl in question has not previously engaged in sexual relations, or it would have used the word used to refer to an immoral woman.

The Septuagint Greek translators of the Old Testament who in 285 B.C. were much closer to the nuances of the original Hebrew, chose to translate the word *almah* as the Greek word *parthenos*, which clearly indicates a virgin. Centuries before the prophecy of Christ's birth was fulfilled or the disciples wrote the Gospel accounts, these Jewish scholars understood that Isaiah's prophecy declared that the Messiah would be born of a virgin. Furthermore, Isaiah predicted that this birth of the Messiah to an *almah* would be a supernatural "sign" to Israel. If the critics were correct — that Isaiah's prophecy predicted that only a young unmarried girl would give birth to a child through normal sexual relations — the question that arises is this: In what way would such a fairly common event as an unmarried woman having a child out of wedlock be a miraculous "sign" from God to the nation of Israel? Obviously, the "sign" refers to a miraculous virgin birth as confirmed by the New Testament gospels.

Christ's Virgin Birth and the Curse of King Jeconiah

There is a curious feature concerning the genealogy of Jesus recorded in Matthew 1:11: King Josiah of Judah begot his royal son, Jeconiah, and his brothers about the time they were carried away to Babylon. King Jeconiah (also known in the Bible as "Coniah" or "Jehoiachin"), a former king of Judah, was cursed by God for his disobedience. The prophet Jeremiah recorded God's curse against "Coniah" and His eternal decree against this spiritually rebellious king: "Is this man Coniah a despised broken idol? is he a vessel wherein is no pleasure? wherefore are they cast out, he and his seed, and are cast into a land which they know not? . . . *For no man of his seed shall prosper, sitting upon the throne of David, and ruling any more in Judah*" (Jeremiah 22:28–30).

Jesus of Nazareth had a dynastic legal right to the throne of David through his genealogical descent through Jeconiah and His legal adopted father, Joseph, as recorded in the Gospel of Matthew (see chapter 18, "The Mystery of the Two Genealogies of Jesus"). Jeremiah's prophecy declared that no seed or biological descendent of this evil King Jeconiah would ever sit upon the throne of David. However, this prophecy of Jeremiah 22:30 about the exclusion of the biological descendants of King Jeconiah from the throne of David, which included his descendant Joseph, the husband of Mary, made it essential that the Gospels prove that Jesus was not the biological son of His legal father Joseph.

Jesus' biological right to the throne of Israel depended upon His descent from King David as demonstrated through the genealogical lines through many generations extending from King David to His mother Mary. Since Mary was descended from the royal line of David's son Prince Nathan, which did not include King Jeconiah, her biological son Jesus is clearly qualified to sit on the throne of David and rule as Israel's promised Messiah. Therefore Luke's genealogy, which verifies Jesus' birth to Mary and her genealogical descent from Prince Nathan through King Solomon and King David, provides absolute legal proof of Jesus' right to sit on the throne of David as Israel's Messiah. Significantly, during the four decades following Christ's death until the destruction of the Second Temple and its extensive genealogical records, none of the Jewish critics of Jesus Christ ever claimed that his genealogical records did not

The Sistine Madonna. Painting by Raphael.

support His claim to be the legitimate successor to the throne of King David.

The Theological Reasons for Jesus' Virgin Birth

It was necessary that Jesus be born of a virgin for a number of theological reasons, in addition to the obvious need to fulfill the prophecies of Genesis 3:15 and Isaiah 7:14, as discussed earlier. We cannot explain the perfect sinlessness of Jesus of Nazareth unless we accept that He was supernaturally conceived through the Virgin Mary, through the supernatural power of the Holy Spirit, thereby avoiding the original sin of a human father.

While many critics of Christianity have criticized the Gospels' account of the Virgin Birth of Jesus as an unbelievable event, those who accept the existence of God and His purposeful supernatural intervention in human affairs find the biblical account credible. Job wrote about God's overwhelming supernatural power, "I know that Thou canst do everything" (Job 42:2). The Virgin Mary accepted the truth of the angel Gabriel's remarkable announcement that she was about to supernaturally become the mother of a son named Jesus without having intimate relations with a man. She said, "For with God nothing shall be impossible. . . . Be it unto me according to thy word" (Luke 1:37–38). Obviously, if God created the universe, He could produce the virgin birth of Jesus of Nazareth.

If we try to intellectually explain the Virgin Birth of Christ, we find ourselves facing a wall. However, if any critic attempts to deny the physical truth regarding this vital miracle about the Virgin Birth of Christ, he must also deny the supernatural nature of Christianity. Anyone who rejects the Virgin Birth has placed himself outside the historic and orthodox faith of those who accept the truth of Christianity as presented in the New Testament. The Virgin Birth of Christ is not some side issue of the Christian faith; it is fundamental to the orthodox belief of our Christian faith in Jesus Christ.

The Bible reveals that all of humanity since the Garden of Eden has been infected with the evil spiritual fruit that flows from the disobedient, original sin of our first parents, Adam and Eve. Therefore it is essential that the Messiah Himself be personally free from the contaminating influence of spiritual sinfulness. The Holy Spirit overshadowed Mary and miraculously created a fusion of deity and humanity producing the man-child Jesus who came to earth as the Son of God as well as the Son of Man. The Holy Spirit united the Lord's two natures, human and divine. Jesus Christ alone was totally free of sin, and of our original sinful nature inherited from our first father Adam. If Jesus were naturally born as a descendent of Adam, He would have inherited Adam's original sin. If Jesus was born naturally to a human father, he personally would have needed to be redeemed from hell despite His personal sinless life. However, through the grace and plan of God, Jesus Christ was born of a virgin, inherited no guilt, and therefore needed no regeneration from sin.

The Testimony of the Bible

There is a great deal of evidence from the New Testament, as well as manuscripts found in early Church histories, that confirm the events in the earliest years of the Christian faith. The Gospels contain abundant witness to the widespread knowledge of the Virgin Birth of our Lord.

Matthew

Matthew recorded the Virgin Birth in his gospel as follows:

> And she shall bring forth a son, and thou shalt call his name Jesus: for he shall save his people from their sins. Now all this was done, that it might be fulfilled which was spoken of the Lord by the prophet, saying, Behold, a virgin shall be with child, and shall bring forth a son, and they shall call his name Emmanuel, which being interpreted is, God with us. Then Joseph being raised from sleep did as the angel of the Lord had bidden him, and took unto him his wife: And knew her not till she had brought forth her firstborn son: and he called his name Jesus. (Matthew 1:21–25)

In an earlier passage, Matthew also alluded to the supernatural Virgin Birth of Jesus when he wrote concerning the genealogy of Christ: "And Jacob begat Joseph the husband of *Mary, of whom was born Jesus*, who is called Christ" (Matthew 1: 16). This statement of Matthew about "Mary, of whom was born Jesus" clearly refers to the supernatural birth of Jesus to Mary. It is also interesting that, in opposition to Middle Eastern customs, the Magi make no mention of Joseph, nor do they focus their attention upon him, which would be natural if they believed Joseph was the natural father of the newborn King. Clearly Matthew knew of Isaiah's prophecy (Isaiah 7:14) and was in a position to confirm the fulfillment of Isaiah's ancient prophecy in the Virgin Birth of Mary's son Jesus.

Luke

The physician Luke also wrote recording the Virgin Birth of His Lord Jesus of Nazareth. The angel addressed Mary and declared, "Behold, thou shalt conceive in thy womb, and bring forth a son, and shalt call his name Jesus. He shall be great, and shall be called the Son of the Highest: and the Lord God shall give unto him the throne of his father David: And he shall reign over the house of Jacob for ever; and of his kingdom there shall be no end. Then said Mary unto the angel, How shall this be, seeing I know not a man?" (Luke 1:31–34). A further confirmation of this unusual circumstance is found in the words of Luke's Gospel referring to the beginning of the ministry of our Lord as well as to His supernatural birth. "Jesus himself began to be about thirty years of age, being (as was supposed) the son of Joseph, which was the son of Heli" (Luke 3:23). As a physician, Luke certainly knew how remarkable his account of Jesus' birth was to his readers.

John and Mark's Silence

Critics of the Virgin Birth have claimed that the silence regarding this supernatural event in the Gospels of Mark and John provide evidence that these writers did not accept this claim. However, the prophecies of Genesis 3:15 and Isaiah 7:14 clearly predicted the Virgin Birth, and Matthew and Luke both clearly record this miracle in definite language. The reason for John and Mark's silence is obvious: The gospels of Matthew and Luke already made this claim public, and the sensitive and delicate nature of the subject was one that did not need additional repetition. If John and Mark had not believed in the Virgin Birth, they would have questioned it, but they did not. Mark begins his Gospel with a statement that Jesus is "the Son of God," clearly implying the Virgin Birth: "The beginning of the gospel of Jesus Christ, the Son of God" (Mark 1:1). John's Gospel begins with a similar statement: "And the Word was made flesh, and dwelt among us, (and we beheld his glory, the glory as of the only begotten of the Father,) full of grace and truth" (John 1:14). John's choice of phrase, "the Word was made flesh," and his assertion that Jesus of Nazareth is "the only begotten of the Father" clearly acknowledge the supernatural birth of Jesus of Nazareth.

The Apostle Paul

Other critics have pointed to the silence of the apostle Paul regarding the Virgin Birth. As a friend and fellow missionary of Luke, Paul was obviously well aware of the Virgin Birth account found in Luke's Gospel. Another significant indication of Paul's knowledge of the supernatural nature of Christ's birth to Mary is found in his letter to the Galatians, in which he wrote, "But when the fulness of the time was come, God sent forth his Son, *made of a woman*, made under the law" (Galatians 4:4). Why would Paul write that Jesus was "made of a woman" unless he was referring to the well-known fact within the early Church that Jesus was born supernaturally to Mary when she was a virgin?

Conclusion

Although it is impossible to know scientifically how God supernaturally brought about the miraculous conception of Jesus within the virgin womb of Mary, the compelling evidence from the Gospels, as well as Paul's letter to the Galatians, strongly supports the fact that Jesus was truly born to His virgin mother Mary exactly as the Church has claimed for two thousand years.

18

The Two Genealogies of Jesus

Many people have noted that the Gospel of Matthew and the Gospel of Luke provide two very different genealogical tables listing the ancestors of Jesus of Nazareth. The differences are far too great to be explained as a scribe's error in transcription. Some scholars have claimed that there is a real contradiction between these two genealogies of Christ. There is certainly a mystery here that is worthy of exploration.

The Old Testament prophets stated emphatically that the promised Messiah would descend directly from the line of King David (1 Chronicles 17:14). The Jewish people would never have accepted anyone who presented himself as Israel's Messiah without documented proof of his proper lineage from King David. Two of the Gospels, Matthew and Luke, begin their history of the life of Jesus with a detailed genealogy, proving His right to claim to be the King of Israel. If the Herodian royal line had been overthrown, Jesus of Nazareth was probably the only person who could have proven, with reference to the genealogical records preserved in the Temple in Jerusalem, that He had the right to assume the throne of David. Eusebius, an historian of the early Church, recorded in his *Ecclesiastical History* that the Roman Emperor Domitian interviewed the surviving grandsons of Jesus' brother Jude to assure himself that they would not pose a threat to Rome's rule by claiming they were Jewish royalty. The relatives demonstrated by their calloused hands that they were only poor farmers and were set free.

Why are there two different genealogies? Over the last two thousand years, many Bible students have puzzled over these apparent discrepancies. The differences in the way Matthew and Luke record the lineage of Christ needs to be resolved in order to avoid confusion and explain the mystery. In Matthew's Gospel, Jesus' royal line is traced back to King Solomon, the son of King David. In Luke's Gospel, His royal descent is traced back to Solomon's elder brother, Prince Nathan, who was also a son of King David.

It is important to note that during Jesus' life, and for 250 years thereafter, there is no historical evidence that anyone ever questioned His genealogical right to the throne of David. If there truly was a real (rather than an apparent) problem with regard to the different accounts of His genealogy as recorded by Matthew and Luke, surely His Jewish enemies would have challenged the accuracy of the Gospel accounts. The Jewish people at the time of Christ had access to the official genealogical records, which were available for legal examination in the Temple until its destruction by the Roman armies in A.D. 70. The silence of the ancient critics on this score clearly suggests that they understood the two different accounts of His genealogy were complementary, not contradictory.

Matthew Records Jesus' Royal Claim Through His Legal Father, Joseph

And Jacob begat Joseph the husband of Mary, of whom was born Jesus who is called Christ (Matthew 1:16).

The genealogy recorded in Matthew 1:1–17 shows that Jesus had the legal right to the throne of King David through his legal descent from King Solomon, the son of David. Beginning with Abraham, Matthew traces this royal descent through King Solomon ultimately to Joseph, the legal father of Jesus. Jesus attained His legal inheritance of the right to the Jewish throne from his legally presumed father (just as though he had been legally adopted by Joseph). If it were not for this need to prove his legal right to the throne of David through Joseph, God could have chosen a virgin who never married to be the mother of Jesus.

Luke Records Jesus' Royal Claim Through His Natural Mother, Mary

> And Jesus Himself began to be about thirty years of age, being (as was supposed) the Son of Joseph, which was the son of Heli . . . (Luke 3:23–24).

The historian Luke details Christ's genealogy through Mary, recording His ancestors all the way back to Adam. Both Matthew's and Luke's genealogies are identical for the long period between Abraham and King David. However, from King David until Jesus, the genealogy of Luke differs from Matthew in all but three names. Therefore, Luke must be listing Mary's ancestors, not Joseph's ancestors. Luke records the legal line of descent of Jesus through Prince Nathan, the older brother of Solomon, and a royal son of King David (2 Samuel 12:24), and ends with Heli, the father of Mary, the biological mother of Jesus.

Another apparent contradiction in Matthew and Luke is the identity of Joseph's father. Matthew 1:16 states, "And Jacob begot Joseph." Luke 3:23 states: "Joseph, which was the son of Heli." Matthew 1:16 identifies Joseph as the natural, "begotten" (biological) son of Jacob. The word *begat* means "to biologically be the father." Yet Luke records that Joseph was the "legal" son of Heli. The solution to this problem is found by understanding that the original Greek word *nomizo* (which Luke uses in 3:23) means "to lay down a thing as law; to hold by custom, or usage; to reckon correctly, take for granted." Luke's genealogy indicates that Joseph (through his marriage to Mary) was the "legal" son-in-law of Heli, who was the natural father of Mary. Note that Luke does not say that Heli "begat" Joseph. Since Joseph was known as the natural son of Jacob, as recorded in Matthew, it is clear that Luke's choice of the word *nomizo* (as reckoned by custom and law) was carefully chosen to emphasize that Joseph was legally listed in the royal line of descent also, as a result of his marriage to Mary.

Since the genealogical records of Israel were lost when the Roman legions burnt the Temple in August A.D. 70, no one else is able to provide legal evidence that Jesus' ancestry traces back to King David. Therefore, Jesus of Nazareth is the only one who can prove He has a legal right to sit on the throne of David as Israel's Messiah.

19

The Star of Bethlehem

Many scholars over the centuries have attempted to understand the mystery of how the Star of Bethlehem guided the Magi on their five-hundred-mile-long trip from Persia to Jerusalem and then to the tiny village of Bethlehem some six miles to the south of the Holy City. Numerous astronomical events have been proposed as the answer to what occurred in the heavens to actually alert the Magi that something extraordinary was about to occur in the land of Judah.

Fifteen centuries earlier, the pagan prophet Balaam had prophesied under the Spirit of the Lord about Israel's destiny. "I shall see him, but not now: I shall behold him, but not nigh: there shall come a Star out of Jacob, and a Sceptre shall rise out of Israel, and shall smite the corners of Moab, and destroy all the children of Sheth" (Numbers 24:17). Since millions of Jews still lived in the area of ancient Babylon (present-day Iraq and Iran) during the centuries following the Babylonian Captivity, it is quite possible that the Persian Magi were familiar with the

Holy Scriptures of the Jews and knew that the fulfillment of the prophecy, that "a star [will come] out of Jacob," would be the signal that announced the coming of the Messiah king.

The Gospel of Matthew contains the remarkable account of the Magi's journey to Jerusalem in search of the "King of the Jews." Matthew wrote, "Now when Jesus was born in Bethlehem of Judaea in the days of Herod the king, behold, there came wise men from the east to Jerusalem, saying, Where is he that is born King of the Jews? for we have seen his star in the east, and are come to worship him" (Matthew 2:1–2).

The question is this: What did the Magi mean by their statement, "we have seen his star in the east" when they explained why they had traveled five hundred miles westward to visit this newborn "King of the Jews?" The Revised Standard Version translation of Matthew 2:2 renders the Magi's phrase as "we saw the star at its rising" (when it first appeared), which makes sense because the wise men immediately began traveling across the desert toward the land of Judah.

Centuries ago, many believed that God actually maneuvered a celestial body, a "star," to a position so near the earth that it hovered in the sky close to the planet as to directly lead the Magi step by step from Persia to Israel. However, this suggestion is impossible. If God actually moved a star so close to the earth that it would indicate the precise direction the Magi should travel, this proximity would naturally destroy our solar system and all life on our planet.

Other theories have proposed that a new star, a supernova explosion, appeared in a constellation associated with Israel. In support of this theory, Professor Nick Strobel of the University of Washington, Astronomy Department, reports that ancient scientific records written by Chinese astronomers record the appearance of a new star, likely a supernova, within the constellation Capricorn in March and April of 5 B.C.[1] The Chinese astronomers reported that the phenomenon remained visible for more than seventy days. Another theory has been proposed by Dr. Bulmer Thomas of the Royal Astronomical Society[2], he reports that two astronomical events occurred in the period immediately prior to the time most scholars believe King Herod died, following the birth of Jesus. The first astronomical event happened in May 7 B.C., so that there was a conjunction between two planets, Jupiter and Saturn, when they appeared very close together in the heavens. Nine months later, in September 6 B.C., there was another near conjunction of three planets—Mars, Jupiter, and Saturn—that would have been quite visible to the naked eye. The ancients often referred to the planets as "a wandering star" because these bright celestial objects appeared to "wander" in their orbits in comparison to the relatively stationary stars. Therefore, the Magi's reference to a "star" does not exclude the possibility that they were actually referring to a planet, a "wandering star."

We need to understand the motivation and reasoning of the Magi. The Persian Magi were not astronomers in the modern sense of the word, men who spent their lives observing the stars. Rather, the Magi were mathematicians and pagan astrologers who spent almost all of their time calculating horoscopes and relatively little time examining the actual stars in the heavens. Almost all past attempts to understand the Star of Bethlehem phenomenon have focused on the mystery from the viewpoint of modern astronomers, looking at what they might find notable in the stars in the night sky of Judea two thousand years ago. However, this approach is not very useful, in light of the fact that the Persian Magi were not primarily concerned with observational astronomy concerning stars. If we wish to understand how the Magi followed the Star of Bethlehem, we must try to look at the sky though the eyes of the Magi themselves. What planetary events were transpiring in the Zodiac, and particularly in the constellation Aries, and what significance might a Persian Magi attach to these phenomena?

Astrology is clearly not an empirical science and is strongly condemned by the teachings of the Word of God because it is an attempt to prophesy future events using occult practices. However, if one wishes to understand the events surrounding the Bethlehem Star, one must combine an understanding of both astrological and astronomical insights in order to determine the probable celestial events that prompted the Magi to make their arduous journey to

Following the Star. Painting by Gustave Doré.

Jerusalem, and then to Bethlehem, to visit the One who was to be born as the King of the Jews.

The students of astronomy (and astrology) as practiced by the Medes and the followers of the ancient religion of Zoroastrianism of Persia were not concerned with the stars and galaxies that make up the universe. The ancient sages were interested only in the major planets that made up the visible solar system and the movements of these celestial bodies as they orbited against the background of the fixed stars. The sages in the distant past had observed the stars in the heavens and had quite imaginatively divided the heavens into a series of twelve constellations, or star patterns. The twelve constellations that were of primary interest to the astronomers/astrologers were those constellations through which the ecliptic, or the path of the planets in their rotation around the sun (or the Earth as was then believed), passed. The only planets that were known to the ancient world were obviously those celestial objects that were visible with the naked eye: Mercury, Venus, Mars, Saturn, and Jupiter. In addition to these planets, the sun and moon were considered as significant celestial portents. The twelve constellations that appear along the ecliptic were known as the Zodiac, beginning with the constellation Aries. According to a text entitled, *Tetrabiblos*, by Greek scholar Claudius Ptolemy (A.D. 137) the constellation of Aries was clearly associated during the time of Christ with the Jews and the nation of Judea.[3]

The part of the sky identified as the constellation of Aries, otherwise known as the Ram, that lies between the constellations of Taurus and Pisces is a relatively dim area of sky with relatively few bright stars observable to the naked eye. It is probable that the Persian Magi observed some unusual astronomical event within the constellation of Aries that they concluded was a supernatural sign of some great event soon to transpire in the land of Judah.

Michael R. Molnar wrote *The Star of Bethlehem: The Legacy of the Magi,* which explains that astronomical events such as comets and supernova were of little or no interest to the Magi. They were interested in the positions and conjunctions of the planets, sun, and moon against the background of the twelve constellations in the Zodiac.[4]

If Jesus Christ was born as early as 6 B.C., as believed by some theologians and historians, then the following astronomical phenomenon might explain the account of the Magi. On April 17, in 6 B.C., a remarkable conjunction of celestial bodies occurred within twenty-four hours within the constellation of Aries. The sun, moon, Venus, and Jupiter all appeared within the constellation of Aries, associated with the land of Judah. This remarkable celestial event might have alerted the Magi to the fact that something unusual was about to happen in Judah.

The majority of scholars suggest that Jesus was born approximately 4 B.C. This conclusion relied primarily upon the statements of the contemporary Jewish historian Flavius Josephus in his book *Antiquities of the Jews* regarding "an eclipse of the moon" that occurred only four weeks before the death of King Herod.[5] Josephus stated that Herod's death occurred after the lunar eclipse, but before that year's Passover. In the nineteenth century, scholars knew that a lunar eclipse occurred on March 12/13, 4 B.C., and naturally concluded that this fact required the revision of the assumed date of Christ's birth from 1 B.C. to 4 B.C. However, the clear chronology given to us in the Gospel of Luke points to 1 B.C. as the correct date for Christ's birth.

There is additional astronomical and historical evidence that strongly suggests that Jesus was actually born in the tradition year 1 B.C. Astronomers have discovered that another lunar eclipse occurred on January 9, 1 B.C. This lunar eclipse in 1 B.C. is almost certainly the correct year for King Herod's death and the birth of Jesus Christ, as it agrees with all of the secular and biblical evidence. A 1966 study by Professor William Filmer that was published in *Oxford's Journal of Theological Studies* also concluded that King Herod's death definitely occurred in 1 B.C.[6]

It is important to note that a similar conjunction of planets occurred in the constellation Aries during 1 B.C. that might have alerted the Magi to the unfolding events in Judah concerning the birth of the one destined to be king.

However, there is another question that remains to be answered: How did the "star" lead the wise men from King

Herod's palace in Jerusalem to the actual birthplace of Jesus in the small town of Bethlehem just south of the Holy City? The Magi traveled five hundred miles to Jerusalem following "the star" because they believed that something extraordinary was about to occur in the land of Judah. Matthew's Gospel records that after meeting King Herod, the Magi then followed the "star" to Bethlehem, only six miles to the south-southwest of Jerusalem. Many readers of the Scriptures have puzzled over the question of how the star could have directed their attention to Bethlehem when the small village was so close to Jerusalem.

As the Magi left King Herod's presence in Jerusalem, they would have been able to observe the planet Jupiter in the constellation Aries, which would have appeared in the south-southwestern sky, the precise direction they must travel to the small town of Bethlehem, the city of David. In addition to the wise men's observations of the heavens, they asked King Herod, "Where is he that is born King of the Jews?" This question strongly suggests that the Magi were Gentiles. Any Jewish scholar would have known about the prophecy of Micah and would also have wanted to avoid risking the jealous wrath of King Herod by informing him that "the King of the Jews" had been born to replace him. When Herod demanded that his advisors tell him the truth, they immediately referred to the prophecy of Micah 5:2. "But thou, Beth-lehem Ephratah, though thou be little among the thousands of Judah, yet out of thee shall he come forth unto me that is to be ruler in Israel; whose goings forth have been from of old, from everlasting." After King Herod learned the truth about Micah's prophecy he instructed the Magi as follows, "And he sent them to Bethlehem, and said, Go and search diligently for the young child; and when ye have found him, bring me word again, that I may come and worship him also" (Matthew 2:8).

While we cannot be certain at this time as to which of these explanations is correct, we do know that the wise men were motivated to leave their homes to seek the Christ Child in order to worship Him. Those who are wise still seek Him.

Notes

1. Nick Strobel, Internet: http://www.astronomynotes.com/history/bethlehem.star.html

2. Thomas Bulmer, Internet: http://physics.hallym.ac.kr/education/stellar/strobel/history/bethlehem.star.html

3. Claudius Ptolemy, *Tetrabiblos* (Boston: Harvard University Press, 1940).

4. Michael R. Molnar, *The Star of Bethlehem: The Legacy of the Magi* (Camden, N.J.: Rutgers University Press, 1999).

5. Flavius Josephus, *Antiquities of the Jews*, book 17, chapter 6, section 4.

6. William Filmer, "The Chronology of the Reign of Herod the Great," *Oxford's Journal of Theological Studies*, 1966.

20

The "Three Days and Three Nights" Between Christ's Crucifixion and Resurrection

I have been asked hundreds of times about the mystery of the "three days and three nights" in connection with the death and resurrection of Jesus. Many people have naturally asked the question: How can Christ's crucifixion on Good Friday afternoon and His resurrection early Sunday morning be the precise fulfillment of the prophecy of Jesus that His time in the grave would be "as Jonas was three days and three nights in the whale's belly; so shall the Son of man be three days and three nights in the heart of the earth" (Matthew 12:40)? There is obviously a deep mystery involving the chronology of the crucifixion and resurrection of Jesus Christ. My research confirms that the difficulty here is an "apparent" contradiction, rather than a real contradiction.

The Bible repeatedly declares that Jesus was crucified on the Feast of Passover, the feast day that followed the Passover Supper, which had occurred the night before. The fourteenth of Nisan, the evening of the Passover Supper, occurred on Thursday night in A.D. 32, the year of Christ's death. Since Jesus and His disciples participated in the official Passover Supper, they would have sacrificed a lamb from the Temple for their celebration during the late Thursday afternoon of the fourteenth of Nisan with all other Jews in Jerusalem. Jesus was arrested later that night and was tried by the Sanhedrin religious court and by the Roman governor, Pontius Pilate, through the night and early morning. The next day, Friday, was the Feast of Passover, and Jesus was crucified during the afternoon. The Gospels record that Jesus rose from the dead early Sunday morning: "Now when Jesus was risen early the first day of the week" (Mark 16:9).

Some writers believe Jesus should have been in the tomb at least 72 hours to fulfill the "three days and three nights." But the Scriptures repeatedly predicted that Jesus would rise on the "third day," not on the fourth day. "From that time forth began Jesus to shew unto his disciples, how that he must go unto Jerusalem, and suffer many things of the elders and chief priests and scribes, and be killed, and be raised again the third day" (Matthew 16:21). Additional Scriptures confirming that Jesus would rise the "third day" include Matthew 17:23, Mark 9:31, and Luke 9:22. The following scriptural passages confirm that Jesus did rise the "third day" in fulfillment of these specific prophecies: Luke 24:46, John 20:1, Acts 10:40, and 1 Corinthians 15:4.

There is a logical resolution to this apparent contradiction. The ancient Jews counted time in the same inclusive way that British criminal courts count time today. The ancient Jews and our modern British courts include any part of one day as counting as a whole day for the purposes of calculating a judicial sentence. For example, take the case of a prisoner who was sentenced to three days (and nights) in jail for some traffic offence by a judge late on Friday afternoon. If the prisoner was placed in prison on Friday evening at 6:00 P.M., he would be released on Sunday morning at 8:00 A.M., having served his full "three days" (and three nights). The time from late Friday afternoon until midnight would count as one full judicial day. All day Saturday counted as day two. The time from Sunday at 12:01 A.M. until they open the jail doors to release the prisoner at 8:00 A.M. would count as a complete day three. Even though the prisoner had only been in jail for approximately thirty-eight hours, the courts would treat this period as legally three full days of judicial time.

This is the same inclusive manner by which the ancient Jews counted time. Any part of a day counted as a whole day. The Jewish commentary on the Law, the *Talmud*, contains the following comment: "A part of an omah [a day] is equal to an omah." Robert Anderson, a great prophecy writer and the head of Scotland Yard, wrote this comment in his 1895 book, *The Coming Prince:* "In computing time the Jews generally included both the terminal units of a given period."[1]

Therefore, for a Jew living in biblical times such as the prophet Jonah or Jesus of Nazareth, it was normal to speak of a period from Friday afternoon to Sunday morning as being "three days and three nights." Therefore, the Old Testament's account that Jonah was in the belly of the large fish for "three days and three nights" means that the prophet was swallowed at some point on day one, spent the whole of day two inside the fish, and was expelled at some point on day three. This conclusion is confirmed by another Old Testament passage: "And he said unto them, Come again unto me after three days. . . . So Jeroboam and all the people came to Rehoboam on the third day" (2 Chronicles 10:5, 12). If the Jews counted time as we Westerners do, the people would have waited until the fourth day to come to the king. However, they understood the King's expression "after three days" inclusively and came "on the third day" as expected by Rehoboam.

The book of Esther provides additional evidence of the Jewish inclusive method of calculating time. Queen Esther asked her uncle Mordecai to "Go, gather together all the Jews that are present in Shushan, and fast ye for me, and neither eat nor drink three days, night or day: I also and my maidens will fast likewise; and so will I go in unto the king, which is not according to the law: and if I perish, I perish" (Esther 4:16). However, verse 5:1 records that Esther went in to see the Persian king on the third day and did not wait until the fourth day as modern North American readers would count time: "Now it came to pass on the third day, that Esther put on her royal apparel, and stood in the inner court of the king's house." Obviously Queen Esther regarded the traditional Jewish expression "three days and three nights" as a period that began on one day and lasted another full day and ended at some point in time on the third day.

Even the chief priests and Pharisees understood the Lord's prophecy in this Jewish inclusive manner of counting time. The Gospel of Matthew records that these priests approached Pontius Pilate and demanded that his soldiers guard the tomb "until the third day" because they knew about Christ's prophecy that He would rise on "the third day," which was Sunday.

It is certainly significant that not one of the Jewish pagan critics against Christianity during the early centuries of the Church ever raised the "apparent" contradiction of the "three days and three nights." The reason is that all people living in the early centuries of the Christian era clearly understood the expression and calculated time in the same manner as did the ancient Jews.

Notes

1. Robert Anderson, *The Coming Prince* (Grand Rapids: Kregel Publications, 1969) 259.

21

The Darkness at Noon at Christ's Crucifixion

One of the most intriguing biblical mysteries is the account of the supernatural darkness that covered the light from the sun for three hours during the afternoon when Jesus Christ's body hung on the Cross. In the Gospel of Matthew, the disciple records this fascinating miracle: "Now from the sixth hour [12:00 noon] there was darkness over all the land unto the ninth hour [3:00 p.m.]" (Matthew 27:45). The supernatural darkness was also recorded in Mark 15:33 and Luke 23:45. It is a remarkable account because, although it would be impossible for a natural eclipse to occur at that time of year (the Passover feast), three of the Gospel writers recorded this extraordinary miracle, and two Greek pagan historians, Thallus and Phlegon, also recorded the supernatural event in their histories. In this section we will examine the astonishing evidence for one of the greatest miracles ever recorded in the Word of God.

Amos Prophesied a Special Darkness at Noon

Many centuries before the event, the Bible recorded a prophecy that predicted that a day would come when the sun would appear to "go down at noon." The prophet Amos (750 B.C.) lived as a shepherd near Bethlehem in ancient Israel seven centuries prior to the birth of Jesus of Nazareth. The Lord gave him a prophecy to announce to the Jewish people that God would supernaturally cause the sky to darken in the middle of the day as a sign to His people of the divine judgment that was coming to their nation because of their disobedience to God. Amos wrote, "And it shall come to pass in that day, saith the Lord God, that I will cause the sun to go down at noon, and I will darken the earth in the clear day: And I will turn your feasts into mourning, and all your songs into lamentation; and I will bring up sackcloth upon all loins, and baldness upon every head; and I will make it as the mourning of an only son, and the end thereof as a bitter day" (Amos 8:9–10).

Secular Historians Confirm the Darkness at Noon

The Greek Historian Thallus

A very early confirmation of the darkness at noon in connection with the crucifixion of Jesus is found in the writings of the Syrian Greek pagan historian Thallus, in his *Third History*. This account from the middle of the first century is significant because it may have been written close to the time when the Synoptic Gospels were being composed by Matthew, Mark, and Luke, and because it is one of the earliest historical records of an event connected with the crucifixion—the supernatural darkness.

Thallus wrote his historical book in Syria in A.D. 52, only twenty years after the resurrection of Christ. Thallus wrote that darkness totally covered the land at the time of the Passover in the year we now call A.D. 32. Julius Africanus, a North African Christian leader writing in A.D. 215, mentions Thallus' account of the supernatural darkness:

> As to [Jesus'] works severally, and His cures effected upon body and soul, and the mysteries of His doctrine, and the resurrection from the dead, these have been most authoritatively set forth by His disciples and

apostles before us. On the whole world there pressed a most fearful darkness; and the rocks were rent by an earthquake, and many places in Judea and other districts were thrown down. This darkness, Thallus, in the third book of his History, calls as appears to me without reason, an eclipse of the sun. For the Hebrews celebrate the passover on the 14th day according to the moon, and the passion of our Saviour falls on the day before the passover; but an eclipse of the sun takes place only when the moon comes under the sun.[1]

Julius Africanus explained that Thallus' theory for the three hours of darkness was unreasonable because an eclipse of the sun cannot occur at the same time there is a full moon. The moon is almost diametrically opposite the sun during the full moon, which would make a solar eclipse impossible at Passover. Though his explanation was certainly wrong, this historical reference to the darkness by the pagan historian Thallus confirms the Gospel account regarding the miraculous darkness that covered the earth when Jesus was dying on the cross.

There are other ancient historical references to the supernatural darkness that occurred at the death of Christ. Modern astronomers confirm that Julius Africanus was right in his conclusion that a normal eclipse could not possibly occur at the time of a full moon, which did occur at the time of the Jewish Passover. The Jewish high priest carefully calculated the position of the full moon to the smallest degree, because their whole liturgical calendar, especially the feast of Passover, depended on determining the precise lunar position. There are two important points here. First, Thallus, who was alive at the time of Jesus' death, confirmed that darkness covered the earth at the exact time recorded by the Gospels. Second, the fact that there was a full moon present makes it certain that this darkness was not an eclipse, but rather that it was a supernatural event.

The Greek Historian Phlegon

A second remarkable historical reference to this supernatural darkness is found in the manuscript of another pagan historical writer originally from Lydia named Phlegon, a Greek who was granted freedom as a Roman citizen by the Emperor Adrian. Phlegon lived in Tralles, a town in Asia Minor near Ephesus. In approximately A.D. 138, Phlegon noted the astonishing fact that this "great and extraordinary eclipse of the sun distinguished among all that had happened" occurred "in the fourth year of the two hundred and second olympiad," which was the nineteenth year of the reign of Tiberius Caesar as emperor of Rome (the year A.D. 32 on our calendar, the year of Christ's death). In his *Chronicle* (A.D. 300), the Christian historian Eusebius quoted from Phlegon's sixteen-volume *Collection of Olympiads and Chronicles* as follows:

> All which things agree with what happened at the time of our Saviour's passion. And so writes Phlegon, an excellent compiler of the Olympiads in his thirteenth book, saying: "In the fourth year of the two hundred and second olympiad there was a great and extraordinary eclipse of the sun, distinguished among all that had happened before. At the sixth hour the day was turned into dark night, so that the stars in the heavens were seen, and there was an earthquake in Bithynia which overthrew many houses in the city of Nice." So writes the above named author.[2]

Furthermore, Phlegon indicated that the darkness that covered the earth began at the sixth hour, which is equivalent to 12:00 A.M., our noon hour—at precisely the same hour as recorded in Matthew 27:45.

Another source confirms that the historian Phlegon wrote in his book, *Olympiades*, that an unprecedented darkness and a devastating earthquake occurred at noon, when Jesus Christ was dying on the Cross:

> In the 4th year of the 202nd Olympiad, there was a great eclipse of the Sun, greater than had ever been known before, for at the 6th hour the day was changed into night and the stars were seen in the heavens. An earthquake occurred in Bythinia and overthrew a great part of the city of Nicæa.[3]

The Roman Government Archives

The Christian writer Tertullian (A.D. 160–220) wrote that the event of supernatural darkness was recorded in the official Roman government archives, and that the record could still be consulted in his day. Tertullian wrote a book entitled *Apology.* that defended the Christian faith and the Gospel account of Christ's crucifixion. "At the same time at noonday there was a great darkness. They thought it to be an eclipse, who did not know that this also was foretold concerning Christ. And some have denied it, not knowing the cause of such darkness. And yet you have that remarkable event recorded in your archives."[4]

In discussing the death of Jesus, Tertullian also wrote about the supernatural darkness:

> And yet, nailed upon the cross, He exhibited many notable signs, by which His death was distinguished from all others. At His own free-will, He with a word dismissed from Him His spirit, anticipating the executioner's work. In the same hour, too, the light of day was withdrawn, when the sun at the very time was in his meridian blaze. Those who were not aware that this had been predicted about Christ, no doubt thought it an eclipse. You yourselves have the account of the world-portent still in your archives.[5]

It would have been foolish and counterproductive for Tertullian to have quoted from official Roman archives regarding the supernatural darkness that accompanied Jesus Christ's death unless Tertullian knew that the government archives contained official records about these events.

The Christian martyr and teacher Lucian of Antioch died as a martyr in Nicomedia during the reign of Emperor Maximinus Daza in A.D. 312. Lucian wrote that the Roman Empire's public archives contained a record of this supernatural event that established the miraculous nature of Christ's death on the Cross: "Look into your annals; there you will find that in the time of Pilate, when Christ suffered, the sun was obscured, and the light of the day was interrupted with darkness."

The Penitent Thief. Painting by Gustave Doré.

The official Roman government archives were available in the first few centuries of the Christian era to be studied by scholars and government officials. Every year the governor of every Roman province had to submit an official report to the Roman Senate concerning the wars, laws, taxes, trials, and unusual events that occurred during their watch. In light of the fact that these Christian teachers and writers were attempting to defend their Christian faith against powerful prejudice and opposition, the appeal to their readers to check out the official government account of Jesus Christ's trial in the Roman public archives provides compelling evidence that such official records confirming the mysterious darkness at noon must have existed in their day.

Notes

1. Julius Africanus, *Extant Writings 18, Ante-Nicene Fathers,* Vol. 6. (Grand Rapids: Wm. B. Eerdmans Publishing Co., 1987).
2. Phlegon, *Collection of Olympiads and Chronicles, quoted by Eusebius, Church History, Ante-Nicene Fathers* p. 3–4.
3. C. Muller, *Fragmenta Historicum Græcorum* Vol. 3, 607.
4. Tertullian, *Apology,* trans. *Ante-Nicene Library,* 10 vols. (Grand Rapids: Wm. B. Eerdmans Publishing Co., 1987) vol.3, XXI.
5. Tertullian, *Apology,* trans. *Ante-Nicene Library,* 10 vols. (Grand Rapids: Wm. B. Eerdmans Publishing Co., 1987) vol. 3 XXI.

22

The True Tomb
of Jesus

Although the facts concerning the crucifixion of Jesus Christ and His subsequent burial are among the best-attested historical events in the whole of Scripture, there is a profound mystery concerning the actual location where He was crucified and the tomb where His disciples laid His body. Some may ask why we should care about the location of Christ's tomb. The answer is that the events surrounding Christ's death and resurrection are fundamental to our Christian faith; therefore, it is natural that we should attempt to determine the location of the tomb that held of the body of our Lord until His resurrection. The Bible's claims about Christ are uniquely grounded in the historical events that occurred in definite places at definite times. Unlike the contradictory and unbelievable myths of the ancient world, the Gospels constantly appeal to eyewitness accounts as evidence that its statements are trustworthy.

One of the great mysteries of the Bible is how the location of His tomb could ever have been lost to the Christians living in Jerusalem during the first few centuries following Christ's resurrection. The reason appears to be that the catastrophic destruction of Jerusalem by the Roman legions in A.D. 70 destroyed most of the landmarks of the city. The Gospel of Mark recorded Christ's prophecy that was fulfilled thirty-eight years later: "Seest thou these great buildings? there shall not be left one stone upon another, that shall not be thrown down" (Mark 13:2). Sixty-five years after the Roman legions destroyed the whole city of Jerusalem in A.D. 70, the Roman emperor Hadrian returned to destroy Jerusalem once again following the Jewish Bar Kochba Rebellion in A.D. 135, killing over one million Jewish citizens outside the city of Jerusalem. Emperor Hadrian then ordered that no Jews be allowed to enter Jerusalem or even come within sight of the city. Hadrian then rebuilt the destroyed city, naming it *Aelia Capitolina*. In light of the repeated destruction of Jerusalem and the forced exile of the Jews (including Jewish Christians) from the city for more than a century, the transformed geography of the rebuilt city would make the correct identification of a site such as Christ's tomb very difficult. Naturally, the believers who returned to Jerusalem after Christians were no longer persecuted (Emperor Constantine's Edict of Toleration, A.D. 313) over a century later found it difficult to reconstruct precisely where key historical events had occurred during Christ's death and burial three centuries earlier.

Although we cannot at this point identify Christ's tomb with absolute certainty, the biblical and archeological evidence points toward a particular geographical location in northern Jerusalem. For almost seventeen centuries, the vast majority of Christians have assumed that the true site of Christ's death and burial was the ancient Church of the Holy Sepulchre, one of the oldest churches in Christendom. However, questions about the validity of this location have been raised from time to time due to the location of the Church of the Holy Sepulchre in the center of the walled city of Jerusalem, in contradiction to the biblical description that Jesus was buried outside the city walls. We will examine the evidence in support of the traditional site of Jesus' tomb at the Holy Sepulchre, as well as the alternative possibility that the real tomb was discovered more than a century ago in an ancient garden just north of the wall of the Old City near Jerusalem's Damascus Gate, which is known today as the Garden Tomb.

The Scriptural Account of Christ's Death and Burial

The Gospels contain detailed references about the crucifixion of Jesus at Golgotha and His subsequent burial in a nearby garden tomb owned by of one of His followers, Joseph of Arimathea.

> And they took Jesus, and led him away. And he bearing his cross went forth into a place called the place of a skull, which is called in the Hebrew Golgotha. . . . The place where Jesus was crucified was nigh to the city. (John 19:16–17, 20)

> Now in the place where he was crucified there was a garden; and in the garden a new sepulchre, wherein was never man yet laid. (John 19:41)

> Now when they were going, behold, some of the watch came into the city, and shewed unto the chief priests all the things that were done. (Matthew 28:11)

> Wherefore Jesus also, that he might sanctify the people with his own blood, suffered without the gate. (Hebrews 13:12)

Note that all of the Gospel records and the book of Hebrews quoted above confirm that the location of Christ's death and burial was a place *outside* the walls of Jerusalem.

The Church of the Holy Sepulchre

The Church of the Holy Sepulchre was constructed in A.D. 326 by the newly converted Roman emperor Constantine. His Christian mother, Queen Helena, traveled to Israel and identified numerous key sites associated with the events concerning the life, death, and resurrection of Jesus. Many historic churches were built on these sites. Following Queen Helena's tour, we see the beginning of religious pilgrimage by Christians to visit the holy places connected with the life of Jesus. Helena spoke to a number of

Christian leaders in Jerusalem and chose the location of the Holy Sepulchre primarily based upon their recommendation. There is no historical evidence that the knowledge of the exact location of the Lord's tomb was venerated and successfully passed on from generation to generation following the destruction of Jerusalem until Queen Helena's visit to Jerusalem, when the tomb site was first publicly identified.

One of the strongest reasons in favor of the Church of the Holy Sepulchre being the true site is that for almost seventeen hundred years it has been endorsed as the genuine site of Calvary by untold millions of followers of Christ, including the Roman Catholic Church, the Russian and Greek Orthodox Churches, and several major Protestant denominations.

Difficulties with the Holy Sepulchre Location

Many have puzzled over the fact that the Holy Sepulchre is actually located in the middle of the Old City of Jerusalem, in direct contradiction to the statements found in three of the Gospels that identify the location of Jesus' death and burial as being outside the walls of the city. And there is no evidence whatsoever that the early Christians venerated the site as a holy place during the first three centuries prior to the building of the Church of the Holy Sepulchre in A.D. 326. A writer named St. Willibald (A.D. 800) noted the contradiction, saying that Golgotha "was formerly outside Jerusalem; but Helena, when she found the Cross, arranged that place so as to be within the City of Jerusalem."[1] Another writer, Saewulf, visited Jerusalem in A.D. 1102 and suggested the city was rebuilt so it would now encompass the original location that was formerly outside the walls: "We know that our Lord suffered without the gate. But the Emperor Hadrian, who was also called Aelius, rebuilt the city of Jerusalem, and the Temple of the Lord, and added to the city as far as the Tower of David."[2]

The inescapable and undeniable problem is that the Church of the Holy Sepulchre is located deep within the city of Jerusalem. The defenders of the Holy Sepulchre location for the tomb of Christ suggest that the Second Wall that defended Jerusalem from the north and west must have curved sharply inward to the south from the present Damascus Gate to encompass the site of the Holy Sepulchre. The problem is that there is no archeological evidence that proves the Second Wall was actually located to the east of the Holy Sepulchre, thus contradicting the book of Hebrew's declaration that Christ "suffered without the gate." (See the map of ancient Jerusalem.)

Military men and historians who understand ancient city plans of military defense suggest that it is highly unlikely that any Roman or Jewish military engineer would have ever built a defensive wall for a major city like Jerusalem that would jut deep into the center of the city. Furthermore, such a hypothetical wall would leave the site of the Holy Sepulchre, which was on a considerable hill, just outside and to the north of the city wall. Such an implausible position for a defensive wall would leave the city at the mercy of its enemies, who could attack the wall from the higher ground. It is almost inconceivable that the experienced military engineers of Rome would permit a defensive wall (the hypothetical Second Wall on the map) to be built in a valley that would allow an enemy to easily attack the wall from a higher position.

The New Testament states that Jesus "suffered without the gate" (Hebrews 13:12). However, there is no conclusive historical or archeological evidence that there was ever a major gate near the Holy Sepulchre. The Romans usually crucified their victims on major highways to attract large audiences in order to terrorize the population. There is no archeological evidence that any major road ever existed near the Holy Sepulchre site.

It is significant that Reverend Charles Couasnon, the Catholic expert who directed the restoration of the Church of the Holy Sepulchre site during the 1970s, expressed serious doubt that this site was the authentic place of Christ's tomb: "One cannot actually prove that the present site, which has been considered the authentic one since the year 326, is, beyond any doubt, the same as that venerated by the Christian community in apostolic times."[3]

Significantly the archeologist Col. C. R. Conder rejected the Holy Sepulchre as the genuine site of Golgotha during his 1886 lecture to the Palestine Exploration Fund in London: "I think enough is now known to lead to the conclusion that the traditional site of the Holy Sepulchre must be abandoned and that we are free to accept the site without the walls [Garden Tomb] which Jewish tradition has indicated as the site of Calvary."[4]

Archeologists have determined that King Herod's palace was located only a few hundred yards from the site of the Holy

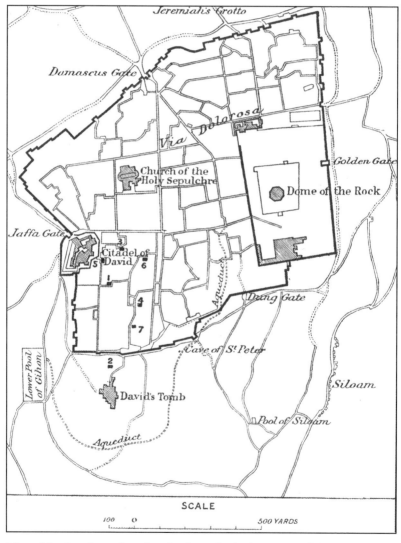

Map of Ancient Jerusalem showing hypothetical position of the Second Wall.

Sepulchre. It defies common sense to believe that King Herod would place a site for public executions so close to his palace. The sounds of the executions and the stench from bodies left on crosses would make it extremely unlikely. Significantly, archeologists examining the Holy Sepulchre did not find a groove for a rolling-stone-type door to seal the tomb entrance, as described in the Gospels.

The Alternative:
Gordon's Calvary and the Garden Tomb

In 1883, General Charles Gordon, a brilliant English military leader, visited Jerusalem and stayed in a house that overlooked the northern wall of the Old City. Looking north out the window of his residence, the general noticed that the hill on the outside of the northern wall bore a startling resemblance to a skull. General Gordon was convinced that the site must be the genuine Calvary. Wealthy Christians in England contributed money to the Garden Tomb Association to purchase the property, which included the Garden Tomb and a strip of land that extended northwest toward the part of the cliff face that included the skull shape. They bought the site a century ago and have preserved it to the present time. Today Jerusalem's main bus terminal sits directly in front of the cliff face of Golgotha, making it difficult for the average visitor to imagine what the site would have looked like in the first century. Fortunately, I have a photograph that was taken in 1890 that shows Golgotha very much as it must have looked two thousand years ago.

One of the strongest reasons for suggesting that the site known as Gordon's Calvary might be the actual location of Golgotha is that this site is outside the ancient and present walls of the Old City of Jerusalem. Also, the location is not far from the Damascus Gate, which has been proven to be the ancient northern gate of the Holy City.

For more than a century archeologists have seriously considered whether this site might be the true site of Christ's crucifixion. There is historical evidence that the site of Gordon's Calvary had been considered from as early as the second century to be the probable site of the execution of the martyr St. Stephen and the prison of Jeremiah before the Temple was destroyed by the Babylonians in 587 B.C. The Jews have traditionally believed that Jeremiah was imprisoned and stoned to death by the nobles of Jerusalem in a cistern prison northeast of the Damascus Gate within a hundred yards of the site of the Garden Tomb. The remains of this ancient cistern can still be seen.

Archeologists recently discovered an ancient tunnel with a very high roof (over 30 feet) that extends all the way beneath the Old City of Jerusalem from the Temple Mount to connect to Solomon's Quarry, the enormous quarried cave beneath the Muslim Quarter of Jerusalem that extends from the Temple Mount all the way north to the Damascus Gate. My wife Kaye and I have explored this tunnel system, as well as Solomon's Quarry, extensively with the assistance of my Israeli contacts. This previously unknown ancient tunnel was used by King Zedekiah to secretly meet with the imprisoned prophet Jeremiah without the knowledge of the Jewish nobles who opposed the prophet's message. The Bible refers to King Zedekiah, his family, and his soldiers' attempt to escape from the Babylonian

The Church of the Holy Sepulchre.

army's siege of Jerusalem in 606 B.C. by secretly traveling along this long tunnel "betwixt the two walls" to a point outside the city walls (Jeremiah 39:4–5; 2 Kings 25:4–5).

Very few cities have ever used two places of execution. The evidence is very strong that this site, known as Gordon's Calvary, was the place of execution of both Jeremiah and St. Stephen, and was known as "the place of stoning." The probability is high that the Romans would have used the same ancient place of execution for the crucifixion of Jesus, since few cities in the ancient world had more than one site for execution.

The site that is now known as the Garden Tomb is located approximately one hundred yards from Gordon's Calvary. Archeologists confirmed that the site was an ancient garden with a rock-cut tomb. They have discovered the remains of a wine press, as well as a huge underground cistern capable of holding more than two hundred thousand gallons of water. These specifications are consistent with a rich man's garden as described in the Gospels. The Scriptures tell us that the garden and the tomb belonged to Joseph of Arimathea, a disciple of Jesus who was also a member of the Jewish religious high court known as the Sanhedrin. In the first century, the town of Arimathea was located just five miles north of the site of the Garden Tomb. Remnants of ritual baths, known as *mikvahs*, were found in the garden. This would also be consistent with a religious leader of the Sanhedrin and his need for ritual cleanliness prior to his visits to the Temple.

The evidence is quite strong that the Romans would have crucified their victims by placing the cross in holes in the ground at the base of the cliff known as Gordon's Calvary, which forms the northern face of the ancient quarry. Such a location would have allowed a large crowd to witness the victims' anguish and hear their agonized cries, because the site is located just outside the ancient Damascus Gate and on the main road that lies north of the city walls connecting Jericho and Jaffa. A Roman writer, Quintillian, described the brutal Roman crucifixions: "Whenever we crucify criminals, very crowded highways are chosen so that many may see it and many may be moved by fear of it; because all punishment does not pertain as much to revenge as to example."[5] The Gospel of Mark confirms that Jesus was crucified close to a road. "And they that passed by railed on him, wagging their heads, and saying, Ah, thou that destroyest the temple, and buildest it in three days" (Mark 15:29).

Over a century ago, a German architect, Dr. Baurath C. Schick, was hired by the Turkish authorities in Jerusalem to complete detailed surveys of the Holy City. He prepared a report for the Palestine Exploration Fund in 1892 documenting his knowledge about the discovery of an ancient tomb only a hundred yards from the site of Gordon's Calvary, but out of direct line of sight, because the cliff curves to the north near that point (as indicated in the map). Dr. Schick explained that a Greek citizen of Jerusalem owned the piece of land to the west of Gordon's Calvary and had discovered this remarkable cave when he removed about five feet of earth and rubbish from his property in 1867. The tomb contained a great deal of earth, as well as a number of skeletons on the surface. When Schick examined the tomb, he found that its bottom was covered with several feet of accumulated dust. This indicated that the tomb

An 1890 Photograph of Golgotha.

had been abandoned for many centuries before some Byzantine Christians (after A.D. 400) reused the empty tomb to bury bodies on top of the earth. The tomb was approximately ten feet long, eight feet wide, and six-and-a-half feet high. There are three steps that lead down to the area where the body would have been laid. It is obvious that the tomb was never fully finished.[6]

One of the most significant facts about the Garden Tomb was that a stone ledge had been cut from the bedrock that runs parallel to the cliff face directly in front of the tomb's entrance (as shown in the photograph). This would be consistent with a groove to guide a rolling stone large enough to completely close the door of the tomb. The width of the stone groove running in front of the Garden Tomb's entrance is identical to the rolling stone found in the first-century-B.C. Tombs of the Kings in northern Jerusalem.

Gordon's Calvary and the Garden Tomb

The cliff face known as Gordon's Calvary superficially resembles the face of a skull. The Garden Tomb's location outside the city walls and near a major city gate as well as an ancient highway, together with a garden tomb very close to Jerusalem's traditional place of execution, strongly favor the site's authenticity as the place of the Lord's burial.

Conclusion

The burden of biblical, historical, and archeological evidence points persuasively toward the Garden Tomb as the probable site of our Lord's burial. Unfortunately, despite a century of further archeological investigation, we still cannot be absolutely certain which of the two sites is the true location of Calvary and the place where Jesus of Nazareth's body was laid. I hope that new excavations will conclusively reveal the true site of Christ's tomb to the satisfaction of all those who are searching for the truth about Jesus.

Notes

1. St. Willibald, *Palestine Pilgrims' Texts,* Vol. iii. (London: 1897).
2. Saewulf, Quoted in Claude Conder's *The Holy Sepulchre,* P.E.F.Q.S. (1883).
3. Charles Couasnon, *The Church of the Holy Sepulchre in Jerusalem* (London: Oxford University Press, 1974).
4. Claude Conder, *Palestine Exploration Fund Statement,* January (1887) 20.
5. Quintillian, Quoted in *Palestine Exploration Fund Report Statement* July (1892).
6. Baurath Schick, *Palestine Exploration Fund Statement* July (1892) 308.

The Garden Tomb. Note the Trough to Guide the Rolling Stone.

23

The Mystery of the 153 Fish

One of the most curious passages in the Bible is the account recorded in the Gospel of John when Jesus met His disciples in Galilee after His resurrection. Jesus directed His disciples to cast their net on the right side of their boat. The fishermen obeyed Christ's instructions and then caught a great "multitude of fishes." However, John included a mysterious statement that has puzzled many readers over the last two thousand years. Strangely, John reported that the "multitude of fishes" amounted to precisely "an hundred and fifty and three."

> Simon Peter saith unto them, I go a fishing. They say unto him, We also go with thee. They went forth, and entered into a ship immediately; and that night they caught nothing. But when the morning was now come, Jesus stood on the shore: but the disciples knew not that it was Jesus. Then Jesus saith unto them, Children, have ye any meat? They answered him, No. And he said unto them, Cast the net on the right side of the ship, and ye

shall find. They cast therefore, and now they were not able to draw it for the multitude of fishes. Therefore that disciple whom Jesus loved saith unto Peter, It is the Lord. Now when Simon Peter heard that it was the Lord, he girt his fisher's coat unto him, (for he was naked,) and did cast himself into the sea. And the other disciples came in a little ship; (for they were not far from land, but as it were two hundred cubits,) dragging the net with fishes. As soon then as they were come to land, they saw a fire of coals there, and fish laid thereon, and bread. Jesus saith unto them, Bring of the fish which ye have now caught. Simon Peter went up, and drew the net to land full of great fishes, an hundred and fifty and three: and for all there were so many, yet was not the net broken. Jesus saith unto them, "ome and dine. (John 21: 3–12)

Why in the world would the disciples count the exact number of fish as being precisely 153? And why would the apostle John then record such a curiously precise number in the Scriptures under the inspiration of the Holy Spirit? Whenever I asked pastors or seminary professors why they thought the Gospel included such an unusually precise number as 153 fish, they invariably responded with a shrug and the comment that they had no idea why the Scriptures included such an obscure detail. However, the Scriptures contain no accidental or extraneous statements. There must be a reason for the mention of "153" fish.

It is interesting to note that Jesus commanded His disciples, "Cast the net on the right side of the ship, and ye shall find" (John 21:6). This reference to the right side clearly implies that those fish that will be caught are "good," as the "right" side appears often in Scripture in reference to that which is good. When Jesus Christ establishes His kingdom He will command His righteous "sheep" as follows: "And he shall set the sheep on his right hand, but the goats on the left. Then shall the King say unto them on his right hand, Come, ye blessed of my Father, inherit the kingdom prepared for you from the foundation of the world" (Matthew 25:33–34). Despite the multitude of "great fishes, an hundred and fifty and three: and for all there were so many, yet was not the net broken" (John 21:12). This well known passage confirms the biblical truth that those who are called and chosen of God will be safe in their salvation. Bishop Richard Trench wrote in his book *Notes on the Miracles of the Lord*, "here the nets are drawn up to land, to the safe and quiet shore of eternity." Referring to the precise number—153 fish—Trench wrote of this, "definite number, even as the number of the elect is fixed and pre-ordained... here they are all 'great,' for all shall be such who attain to that kingdom, being equal to the Angels."[1]

Over the years following my biblical studies in Philadelphia, I consulted dozens of Bible commentaries and numerous theological volumes without finding any satisfactory answer. To my surprise, I finally discovered that this mystery concerning the 153 fish also puzzled some of the important fathers of the early Church in the first few centuries following Christ's resurrection. Augustine of Hippo, a brilliant theologian of the early Church, wrote in his famous book *The City of God* that these fish were certainly a symbol of Christians and the Church. "If you join the initial letters of these five Greek words, 'ιησους Χριστος Θεου υιος σωτηρ, which mean, 'Jesus Christ the Son of God, the Saviour,' they will make the word Χθυς,—that is, 'fish,' in which word Christ is mystically understood."[2]

The early Christians commonly used the symbol of the fish to stand for the Church, as demonstrated by numerous archeological discoveries of ancient Christian monuments. In his commentary *On the Gospel of St. John*, Augustine wrote about the significance of the 153 fish. "All therefore who are sharers in such grace are symbolized by this number [153], that is, are symbolically represented.[3] Another early Christian theologian, Jerome, referred to the deeper meaning of the 153 fish as pointing to the many different types of men and women that Christ gathers together into the net of the Kingdom of God.

The Gospel's mention of precisely 153 fish, instead of using a round number such as "150," "twelve dozen," or "a great multitude" to describe the fishermen's great catch obviously signifies an important truth to the Church. Certainly the symbolic use of fish in the Gospels signified those who were saved by faith in Christ as illustrated by Jesus' own words referring to His precise knowledge of those individuals who place their faith in Him. "And this is the Father's will which hath sent me, that of all which he hath given me I should lose nothing, but should raise it up again at the last day" (John 6:39). Jesus also declared, "Those that thou gavest me I have kept, and none of them is lost, but the son of perdition; that the scripture might be fulfilled" (John 17:12).

It is also noteworthy that the numerical value of the Hebrew letters that compose the name "Sons of God" is equal to 153. Both of the biblical languages, Hebrew and Greek, used letters to depict numbers as well as letters. The ancient Israelites did not use the Arabic numbers (1, 2, 3, etc.) that are used universally today. In biblical times, they used the letters of their Hebrew alphabet to indicate numbers. The first Hebrew letter, א, signified 1; the second letter, ב, stood for 2; the third letter, ג, stood for 3, etc. Thus, the numerical value of the nine Hebrew letters בני האלהים (*Beni Ha-Elohim*) that form the expression "Sons of God" add up to 153.

This alphanumeric language phenomenon is also referred to in a passage in the Book of Revelation, which unveils the mystery of the number and mark of the beast that will be associated with the future world dictator, the Antichrist. "Here is wisdom. Let him that hath understanding count the number of the beast: for it is the number of a man; and his number is Six hundred threescore and six" (Revelation 13:18). John actually wrote the number "666" using three Greek letters, χξς which represented those specific numbers ($\chi = 600$; $\xi = 60$; $\varsigma = 6$). Biblical scholars recognized that the number six was associated with the number of man, as God created man on the sixth day of the creation week. Six hundred sixty-six represents Satan's Antichrist—a superman without God. When the future Antichrist arises to power during the seven-year Tribulation at the end of this age, the tribulation saints living at that time will be able to identify him by adding up the numerical value of the letters that make up his name (in Hebrew or Greek only) to total 666. The Lord provided this prophecy to enable future Tribulation believers to identify the Antichrist and refuse to worship him or give him allegiance by taking his evil mark 666 on their right hand or forehead.

It is fascinating to observe that the number eight is intimately connected in the Scriptures with Jesus Christ. Eight is associated with resurrection in light of the eight human survivors of Noah's flood and the fact that Jesus rose victoriously from the dead on Sunday, the eighth day, following the seventh day, the Sabbath. The New Testament reveals the name Jesus in the Greek language is Ιησοψε whose six Greek letters add up significantly to 888. This number 888 might have been considered a simple coincidence, except for the fact that every one of the names of Jesus found in the Greek New Testament is also divisible by the number 8: Christ = 1480 (185 × 8); Lord = 800 (100 × 8); Our Lord = 1,768 (221 × 8); Savior = 1,408 (176 × 8); Emmanuel = 25,600 (3,200 × 8); Messiah = 656 (82 × 8); and Son = 880 (110 × 8).

In contrast, it is interesting to note that virtually every one of the names associated with Satan and his Antichrist is divisible by 13. For example, in the Hebrew language of the Old Testament the following names of the devil are divisible by 13: Satan = 364 (28 × 13); Beelzebub (with the article) = 598 (46 × 13); Belial = 78 (6 × 13); the piercing Serpent, even Leviathan = 1,170 (90 × 13). In the Greek language of the New Testament: Satan = 2,197 (169 × 13); the man of sin = 1,963 (151 × 13); the son of perdition = 1,807 (139 × 13); Dragon = 975 (75 × 13); Serpent = 780 (60 × 13).

The Bible contains many numbers; several of which are of great significance. The ancient Jews and the surrounding pagan nations were fascinated with the significance of numbers. The Bible itself often refers to the importance of its numbers. David wrote, "He telleth the number of the stars; he calleth them all by their names" (Psalm 147:4). The prophet Isaiah also referred to God numbering the heavenly host. "Lift up your eyes on high, and behold who hath created these things, that bringeth out their host by number: he calleth them all by names by the greatness of his might, for that he is strong in power; not one faileth" (Isaiah 40:26).

A Christian army officer, Lt. Col. R. Roberts, made one of

the most interesting discoveries about this fish passage more than a century ago. He was curious about the reason for the unusual precision of the number of fish—153. Roberts carefully tabulated the following list of 153 individual men and women recorded in the four Gospels who received a direct blessing as a result of their personal encounter with Jesus Christ. Remarkably, Roberts discovered that the four Gospels record precisely 153 individuals who were specifically blessed by Jesus Christ.[4] These divine blessings through their personal encounters with Jesus Christ included salvation, divine healings, resurrections, as well as those persons who were personally blessed through witnessing Christ supernaturally blessing their friend or loved one (such as Jairus and his daughter). It is very unlikely that this number—153—was a simple coincidence. This passage clearly demonstrates that the Lord numbers and personally watches over every individual who places his faith and trust in Him. Jesus noted, "Are not two sparrows sold for a farthing? and one of them shall not fall on the ground without your Father. But the very hairs of your head are all numbered" (Matthew 10:29–30).

153 Individuals Blessed Through Their Encounter with Jesus

Individuals	Reference	People Blessed by Christ
1. The leper	Matthew 8:2–4	1
2. Centurion and servant	Matthew 8:5–13	2
3. Peter's wife's mother	Matthew 8:14–15	1
4. Two possessed with devils	Matthew 8:18	2
5. Palsied man and bearers	Matthew 9:2	5
6. Jairus and his daughter	Matthew 9:18–25	2
7. Woman with issue of blood	Matthew 9:21–22	1
8. Blind men	Matthew 9:27–31	2
9. Dumb man	Matthew 9:32–33	1
10. Eleven Apostles	Matthew 10:1–4	11
11. Man with withered hand	Matthew 12:10–13	1
12. Blind, dumb, devil-possessed	Matthew 12:22	1
13. Brethren of the Lord	Matthew 13:55	4
14. Syro-Ph. woman & daughter	Matthew 15:22–28	2

15. Lunatic child and father	Matthew 17:14–18	2
16. Blind men (leaving Jericho)	Matthew 20:30–34	2
17. Simon the leper	Matthew 26:6	1
18. Mary (sister of Lazarus)	Matthew 26:7	1
19. Centurion	Matthew 27:54	1
20. Salome (wife of Zebedee)	Matthew 27:56	1
21. Mary (wife of Cleopas)	Matthew 27:56	1
22. Mary Magdalene	Matthew 27:56	1
23. Joseph of Arimathea	Matthew 27:57–60	1
24. Man with unclean spirit	Mark 1:23–26	1
25. Man, deaf and dumb	Mark 7:32–35	1
26. Blind man	Mark 8:22–26	1
27. Son of the widow of Nain	Luke 7:12–15	1
28. A woman, a sinner	Luke 7:37–38	1
29. Joanna and Susanna	Luke 8:3	2
30. A disciple—"Follow Me"	Luke 9:59–62	1
31. The seventy disciples	Luke 10:1–9	70
32. Martha	Luke 10:38–42	1
33. Woman with infirmity	Luke 13:11–13	1
34. Man with dropsy	Luke 14:2–4	1
35. Ten Lepers	Luke 17: 12-14	10
35. Blind man (going to Jericho)	Luke 18:35–43	1
36. Zacchaeus	Luke 19:2–6	1
37. Malchus	Luke 22:50–51	1
38. Penitent thief	Luke 23:42–43	1
39. The two disciples at Emmaus	Luke 24:13–32	2
40. Nicodemus	John 3:1–21	1
41. Woman of Samaria	John 4:7–26	1
42. Nobleman and sick son	John 4:46–50	2
43. Impotent man (Bethesda)	John 5:1–9	1
44. Woman taken in adultery	John 8:3–11	1
45. Man born blind	John 9:1–41	1
46. Lazarus	John 11:1–44	1
47. Mary, mother of Jesus	John 19:25	1
Total of Those Personally Blessed by Christ		**153**

Jesus gathered His disciples together to give them guidance and instructions regarding their future mission. He promised His followers that every one of us is of great value to our Father in heaven: "Are not two sparrows sold for a farthing? and one of them shall not fall on the ground without your Father. But the very hairs of your head are all numbered. Fear ye not therefore, ye are of more value than many sparrows" (Matthew 10:29–31).

In fact, the Word of God declares that the Lord is concerned with both the years of our lives and the numbers of our steps: "If a man die, shall he live again? all the days of my appointed time will I wait, till my change come. Thou shalt call, and I will answer thee: thou wilt have a desire to the work of thine hands. For now thou numberest my steps." (Job 14:14–16).

Notes

1. Richard Chenevix Trench, *Notes on the Miracles of Our Lord* (London: Macmillan and Co., 1874) 492-494.
2. Augustine, *The City of God* (Grand Rapids: Wm B. Eerdmans Publishing Co. 1987) xviii: 23.
3. Augustine, *On the Gospel of St. John* (Grand Rapids: Wm B. Eerdmans Publishing Co. 1987) Tractate CXXII.
4. Ethelbert W. Bullinger, *Number in Scripture* (Grand Rapids: Kregel Publications, 1978) 276–278.

24

What Happened to Christ's Disciples?

The lives, ministries, and deaths of Christ's disciples are naturally of great interest to all those who share the Christian faith. However, the New Testament does not provide many details regarding what happened to the apostles after the launch of the church at the Feast of Pentecost. This chapter will attempt to unveil some of the mystery surrounding the lives and deaths of His disciples as martyrs in defense of their faith in Jesus Christ. Although the four Gospels and Paul's Epistles reveal a great deal about the early ministries of several of these great men of God, we are faced with great difficulties when we attempt to determine how and where these disciples died. For the average Christian, it has been very difficult to discover the truth about the lives and martyrdom of the apostles.

Most of our information about the deaths of the apostles is derived from early Church traditions. While ancient tradition is often unreliable as to small details, it very seldom contains outright inventions. Eusebius, the most important of the early church historians, wrote his history of the early church in 325. He wrote, "The apostles and disciples of the Savior scattered over the whole world, preached the Gospel everywhere."[1] Church historians Eusebius and Schumacher researched the lives and deaths of the apostles and recounted the history of their martyrdom.

Matthew preached the gospel message throughout Israel. When he felt led to travel to other lands to preach, he first wrote his Gospel in the Hebrew language so it would remain as an authoritative account of the miracles and words of Jesus Christ. Early Church histories recount that Bartholomew carried a copy of the Hebrew text of Matthew's gospel with him to India in A.D. 52, only twenty years after Christ's Resurrection. Later Matthew's Gospel was translated into the Greek language to enable the Gentiles to read it as well. Matthew reportedly suffered martyrdom in a place called Ethiopia (south of the Caspian Sea, not the Ethiopia in Africa), where he was killed by the sword.

Mark was the constant companion of the apostle Peter. The church tradition is that the early Christians requested that Mark write down all of the words and deeds of Christ as he learned them from his own eyewitness experience, as well as what he learned from his ministry with Peter. The church historian Eusebius states that Mark was the first disciple to travel as a missionary to Egypt, and there he preached his gospel to the Jews and Gentiles in Alexandria.[2] Mark died as a martyr in Alexandria, after being dragged by horses through the streets until he was dead.

Luke, the physician, was born in the great Syrian city of Antioch. He worked with Paul and the other apostles and recorded many eyewitness accounts of the life of Christ. Luke wrote the Gospel of Luke and the book of Acts, which records many of the key events in the early growth of the Church. He was hanged in Greece, as a result of pagan opposition to his tremendous preaching to the lost.

The apostle John traveled to the Roman province of Asia (western Turkey), where he nurtured numerous churches, including those seven churches specifically named in the beginning of the book of Revelation. He was the bishop of these churches in Asia, and had his headquarters in the city of Ephesus, where he finally died at a very old age. John faced martyrdom courageously when he was boiled in a huge basin of boiling oil during the first wave of persecution in Rome under the Emperor Nero. However, he was miraculously delivered from death. Decades later, John was later sentenced to serve in the mines on the prison island of Patmos during the tyranny of Emperor Domitian. At Patmos, John wrote his prophetic book of Revelation.

Eusebius recorded the fact that John had studied and approved the three Gospels as written by Matthew, Mark, and Luke. Eusebius wrote that John "remarked that the narrative only lacked the story of what Christ had done first of all at the beginning of His mission."[3] It is clear that the three Synoptic gospels record the events in Christ's ministry beginning from the point that John the Baptist was imprisoned by King Herod. However, John records the events in Christ's ministry that took place before John the Baptist's imprisonment beginning with Jesus' first miracle at the marriage of Cana: "This beginning of miracles did Jesus in Cana of Galilee" (John 2:11). The apostle John was later freed by the Roman Senate when the emperor died in A.D. 96, and he returned to serve again as Bishop of Edessa. John, as the youngest disciple, lived through the whole of the first century of this eventful era during which the Christian Church flourished against great opposition. He died as a very old man, during the reign of Emperor Trajan (A.D. 98–117), the only one of the apostles to die peacefully in bed.

The apostle Peter preached the Gospel in Pontus, Galatia, Bithynia, Cappadocia, (eastern Turkey), and the province of Asia (western Turkey) to the Jews living in exile from Israel.[4] The Christian writer Clement records the fact that Peter's wife was martyred before his own death. "We are told that when blessed Peter saw his wife led away to death he was glad that her call had come and that she was returning home, and spoke to her in the most encouraging and comforting tones, addressing her by name: 'My dear, remember the Lord.' Such was the marriage of the blessed, and their consummate feeling towards their dearest."[5]

Eventually Peter traveled to Rome, where the Emperor Nero launched the first great wave of persecution against the Christians. The apostle Peter was crucified upside down on an X-shaped cross because, according to early church tradition, he told his pagan tormentors that he felt unworthy to die in the same position that his Lord Jesus Christ had died. The tradition recorded that as Peter was being led to his crucifixion he was heard to say, "None but Christ, none but Christ." Bishop Dionysius of Corinth (A.D. 170) wrote a letter to Soter in Rome in which he discussed the ministry of Peter and Paul in his city of Corinth. "In Italy too they taught jointly in the same city, and were martyred at the same time."[6]

James, the brother of Jesus, came to faith in Christ after His death and resurrection. James is known as "the Just," or "the Righteous." He was elected by the other disciples as the leader of the church in Jerusalem. The early Church leader Clement (Paul's fellow-combatant in the Gospel) wrote, "Peter, James, and John, after the Ascension of the Saviour, did not claim pre-eminence because the Saviour had specially honoured them, but chose James the Righteous as Bishop of Jerusalem."[7] Clement also noted in his book *Outlines*, Book VIII, that James "the Righteous" was thrown over a hundred feet down from the southeast pinnacle of the Temple when he refused to deny his faith in Christ. When his enemies discovered that he miraculously survived the fall, they beat James to death with a fuller's club. This was the same pinnacle of the Temple where Satan had earlier taken his brother Jesus during His time of temptation following His anointing when the Holy Spirit fell upon Him "as a dove."

James the Greater, a son of Zebedee, was a fisherman by trade when Jesus called him to a lifetime of discipleship. As a strong leader of the church, James was ultimately beheaded at Jerusalem. The Roman officer who guarded James watched in amazement as James defended his faith at his trial. Later, the officer walked beside James to the place of execution. Overcome by personal conviction, he declared his new faith in Christ to the judge and knelt beside James as the disciple of Christ accepted beheading with a sword for being a Christian. Clement reported, "So they were both taken away together, and on the way he asked James to forgive him."[8] Luke recorded James' death in the book of Acts. "And he killed James the brother of John with the sword" (Acts 12:2).

Bartholomew, also known as Nathanael, was one of the first disciples to follow Christ. Jesus said of him, "Behold, an Israelite indeed, in whom is no guile!" (John 1:47). Bartholomew was appointed as a missionary to Asia, in present day Turkey. Bartholomew was martyred for his preaching in Armenia (southern Russia), where he was flayed to death by a whip.

Andrew was sent to establish churches in Scythia (southern Russia and the Ukraine), according to Eusebius in his *History of the Church*.[9] Andrew was the brother of Simon Peter and first followed John the Baptist until John directed him to follow Christ. According to tradition, Andrew was crucified on an X-shaped cross at his request. After being whipped severely by seven soldiers, his body was tied to the cross with cords rather than nailed with spikes to prolong his agony. His followers reported that, when he was led toward the cross, Andrew saluted it in these words: "I have long desired and expected this happy hour. The cross has been consecrated by the body of Christ hanging on it." He continued to preach to his tormentors for two days until he expired in A.D. 60, during the reign of the Emperor Nero.

The apostle Thomas was the one disciple who could not accept that Christ had risen from the dead until he personally saw the Lord and placed his fingers in the wound of His side. Thomas was chosen to travel as a missionary to the Parthians (present-day Iraq and Iran) and continued to India, where he established a strong church that still exists today. The soldiers of a pagan king stabbed Thomas to death with spears during his mission trip to India.

The apostle Philip preached the Word of God in Phrygia (central Turkey) and died as a martyr to his faith at Hierapolis in Syria, according to Eusebius' *Church History* Book 5, Ch. 24.

Jude, the brother of Jesus, is reported to have preached the gospel of Christ in Idumea (Jordan), Arabia, and Syria, Egypt, and a long period in Mesopotamia and Persia where it is reported he was slain by the Magi of that land due to his brave declaration of his faith in Jesus in opposition to their pagan superstitions. Jude was killed with arrows when he refused to deny his faith in Christ.

The apostle James, the son of Alpheus, also known as "James the Lessor" to distinguish him from "James the Greater," who was brother of the apostle John and also the son of Zebedee. While the Greek Church tradition speaks of his death as a martyr we have no definite information regarding his death and burial.

Simon the Zealot, also known as the Apostle Simon the Cananite, probably was descended from the ancient pagan peoples of Canaan but his family would have converted to Judaism long before. While the ancient traditions claim he died as a martyr little detail of his ministry or death have survived.

The apostle Thaddeus was sent on a divine mission to the king of Edessa (northern Syria) by the orders of the apostle Thomas. Eusebius relates that the king of Edessa had written a letter to Jesus asking him to come to his city-state and heal him from a terrible disease. However, Jesus reportedly sent a message (observed in the Edessa royal archive by Eusebius around A.D. 310 according to his Church History) to the king and told him He would send a disciple to heal him later. Thaddeus reportedly supernaturally healed the monarch and the result was that Edessa became the first kingdom to become Christian in the first century. There is a tradition in Armenia (south of Russia) that Thaddeus died there as a martyr after preaching to their people.

Matthias the apostle was chosen by lot by the other apostles to replace the traitor Judas Iscariot. He was chosen because he was one of the seventy disciples who could testify as an eyewitness because he had been with Christ as a follower from His baptism by John the Baptist until His ascension. Matthias taught in Jerusalem for several years and was finally stoned and then beheaded as a martyr.

Barnabas was one of the group of seventy disciples, but he was ranked as an apostle. He apparently wrote the *Epistle of Barnabas*. He preached throughout Italy and Cyprus. Church tradition suggests Barnabas was stoned to death at Salonica.

After many years of travel and ministry throughout the

Roman Empire, the apostle Paul was imprisoned and then beheaded during the first major persecution of the Church by the Emperor Nero at Rome in A.D. 67. Paul endured a lengthy imprisonment before his death, which allowed him to write his many epistles to the numerous churches he had formed throughout the Roman Empire. These epistles, which taught many of the foundational doctrines of Christianity, form a significant portion of the New Testament.

Although not every detail can be verified historically, the universal belief of the early Christian writers was that each of Christ's apostles had faced martyrdom faithfully without denying his belief in the resurrection of Jesus Christ. Polycarp, another great leader of the early church, was martyred at the age of eighty-six by being burned alive before an audience of thousands in the amphitheatre in the city of Smyrna. When the Roman governor demanded that the aged bishop deny his faith in Jesus and worship the Roman emperor to save his life, Polycarp refused the invitation to blaspheme Christ and deny his faith with these timeless words: "Eighty and six years have I served Him, and He never did me wrong; and how can I now blaspheme my King who has saved me?"

Notes

1. Eusebius, *The History of the Church, Ante-Nicene Library* 10 vols. (Grand Rapids: Wm. B. Eerdmans Publishing Co., 1987).

2. Eusebius, *The History of the Church*, Book II, chapter 16.*Ante-Nicene Library* 10 vols. (Grand Rapids: Wm. B. Eerdmans Publishing Co., 1987).

3. Eusebius, *The History of the Church*, Book III, chapter 24. *Ante-Nicene Library* 10 vols. (Grand Rapids: Wm. B. Eerdmans Publishing Co., 1987).

4. Eusebius, *The History of the Church*, Book III, chapter 1. *Ante-Nicene Library* 10 vols. (Grand Rapids: Wm. B. Eerdmans Publishing Co., 1987).

5. Clement, *Miscellanies*, Book VII. *Ante-Nicene Library* 10 vols. (Grand Rapids: Wm. B. Eerdmans Publishing Co., 1987).

6. Dionysius, *Letter to Soter*, Quoted in Eusebius, *The History of the Church*, Book II, chapter 26. *Ante-Nicene Library* 10 vols. (Grand Rapids: Wm. B. Eerdmans Publishing Co., 1987).

7. Clement, *Outlines*, Book VI. *Ante-Nicene Library* 10 vols. (Grand Rapids: Wm. B. Eerdmans Publishing Co., 1987).

8. Clement, *Outlines*, Book VII. *Ante-Nicene Library* 10 vols. (Grand Rapids: Wm. B. Eerdmans Publishing Co., 1987).

9. Eusebius, *The History of the Church*, Book III, chapter 1. *Ante-Nicene Library* 10 vols. (Grand Rapids: Wm. B. Eerdmans Publishing Co., 1987).

25

The Mystery of When Miracles and Healing Ceased

For many Christians one of the greatest mysteries is that the tremendous miracles, healings, and supernatural gifts of the Holy Spirit enumerated in 1 Corinthians 12, which characterized the life and worship of the early Church, seem to have ceased by the beginning of the second century. Many theologians have dogmatically asserted that God provided for supernatural miracles and the gifts of the Holy Spirit only to attract the attention of the pagan world and provide divine authority for the introduction of the New Testament as God's inspired revelation. They assert that within a century of Christ's resurrection, all miracles and signs had ceased permanently. Many have claimed that these supernatural signs ceased when the apostles died. Some writers and denominations have asserted this theory as absolute dogmatic truth and reject even the possibility of genuine supernatural miracles occurring today.

Several writers have claimed that a search of the writings of the early Church indicates that there are no references to these "gifts" continuing beyond A.D. 100. However, during the last few years I have carefully examined the writings of the early Church writers from the time of Christ till the Council of Nicea in 325 that were collected in a set of ten volumes known as the *Ante-Nicene Library* and first published in 1890. After an exhaustive search of these fascinating early Christian writings, I can confirm that God continued to manifest His supernatural power including miraculous healings, resurrection from the dead, and demonstrations of charismatic gifts of the Holy Spirit well beyond the age of the apostles. Further research in the writings of the medieval Church provide compelling evidence that miracles, though rare, continued to manifest from time to time in a variety of places as attested by responsible historical authorities.

There are brief references to the prophetic gifts still continuing as reported in the early Church manual known as the *Didache* (A.D. 110). "And every prophet teaching the truth, if he doeth not what he teacheth, is a false prophet. And every prophet approved and found true, if he doeth ought as an outward mystery typical of the Church, and yet teacheth you not to do all that he himself doeth, shall not be judged before you; he hath his judgment in the presence of God; for in like manner also did the prophets of old time."[1]

Bishop Clement's *Letter to the Corinthians,* written by the bishop of Rome (A.D. 100), refers to the continuing supernatural work of the Holy Spirit. "An abundant outpouring also of the Holy Spirit fell upon all."[2] The *Shepherd of Hermas* (A.D. 110) also contains a reference to speaking in tongues and prophecies. "When then the man who hath the divine Spirit cometh into an assembly of righteous men, who have faith in a divine Spirit, and intercession is made to God by the gathering of those men, then the angel of the prophetic spirit, who is attached to him, filleth the man, and the man, being filled with the Holy Spirit, speaketh to the multitude, according as the Lord willeth."[3]

In addition, there are numerous significant references to these supernatural gifts continuing in the life of the early Church in the following centuries.

Irenaeus

The brilliant Christian teacher Irenaeus wrote a treatise against heresies called the *Refutation and Overthrow of Knowledge Falsely So Called* (A.D. 185) that recorded many manifestations of the gifts of the Holy Spirit and supernatural miracles that still continued in some churches, including accounts of people being raised from the dead:

> Some drive out demons really and truly, so that often those cleansed from evil spirits believe and become members of the Church; some have foreknowledge of the future, visions, and prophetic utterances; others, by the laying-on of hands, heal the sick and restore them to health; and before now, as I said, dead men have actually been raised and have remained with us for many years. In fact, it is impossible to enumerate the gifts which throughout the world the Church has received from God and in the name of Jesus Christ crucified under Pontius Pilate, and every day puts to effectual use for the benefit of the heathen, deceiving no one and making profit out of no one.[4]

> Similarly, we hear of many members of the Church who have prophetic gifts and by the Spirit speak with all kinds of tongues, and bring men's secret thoughts to light for their own good, and expound the mysteries of God.[5]

Irenaeus also wrote about the gifts of the Holy Spirit in *Against Heresies*: "In like manner we do also hear many brethren in the church, who possess prophetic gifts, and who through the Spirit speak all kinds of languages, and bring to light for the general benefit the hidden things of men, and declare the mysteries of God." (Irenaeus, *Against Heresies* 5:6:1)

Justin Martyr

Justin Martyr wrote his *Dialogue with Trypho* in A.D. 165 and clearly referred to many supernatural gifts of the Holy Spirit appearing in the daily life of the second-century Church. He wrote, "Daily some of you are becoming disciples in the name of Christ, and quitting the path of error; who are also receiving gifts, each as he is worthy, illumined through the name of this Christ. For one receives the spirit of understanding, another of counsel, another of strength, another of healing, another of foreknowledge, another of teaching, and another of the fear of God."[6]

Tertullian

Tertullian was a major theologian and Christian writer ministering in Carthage. In A.D. 215 he described supernatural visions and prophetic gifts of the Holy Spirit as operating normally in the third-century Church. "And thus we who both acknowledge and reverence, even as we do the prophecies, modern visions as equally promised to us, and consider the other powers of the Holy Spirit as an agency of the Church for which also He was sent, administering all gifts in all, even as the Lord distributed to every one."

Origen

Origen was a Christian theologian who lived and taught in Alexandria, Egypt, from A.D. 185 to 254. In his book *Against Celsus* written in 250, Origen described the gifts of the Holy Spirit as still continuing in the life of the Church. "Traces of the Holy Spirit who appeared in the form of a dove are still preserved among Christians. They charm demons away and perform many cures and perceived certain things about the future according to the will of the Logos."[7]

Origen noted that these charismatic gifts were gradually diminishing, although some "traces of His presence" were still evident. "Moreover, the Holy Spirit gave signs of His Presence at the beginning of Christ's ministry, and after His ascension He gave still more; but since that time these signs have diminished, although there are still traces of His presence in a few who have had their souls purified by the Gospel and their actions regulated by its influence."[8]

Novatian

The Christian theologian Novatian (A.D. 270) of Rome wrote a strong defense of the doctrine of the Trinity and died as a martyr during the second last wave of persecutions by the pagan Roman emperors. Novatian wrote about the key role of the Holy Spirit in supernaturally empowering the Church. "they were henceforth armed and strengthened by the same Spirit, having in themselves the gifts which this same Spirit distributes, and appropriates to the Church, the spouse of Christ, as her ornaments. This is He who places prophets in the Church, instructs teachers, directs tongues, gives powers and healings, does wonderful works, often discrimination of spirits, affords powers of government, suggests counsels, and orders and arranges whatever other gifts there are of charismata; and thus make the Lord's Church everywhere, and in all, perfected and completed."[9]

St. Augustine

Augustine (354–430), bishop of Hippo, was the greatest theologians of the early medieval Church and systematized much of the theology that governed the teaching of the Western Church for over a thousand years. Although in his early years Augustine believed that all miracles had ceased by the end of the lives of the apostles, his view was transformed by the compelling evidence of many well-attested miracles that occurred during a powerful revival that occurred throughout the churches of North Africa that were under his supervision. In the last section of his epic work *The City of God*, Augustine wrote about numerous miracles that he had personally witnessed and investigated, including remarkable miraculous healings involving breast cancer, paralysis, blindness, and even people who were resurrected from the dead. He wrote, "For even now miracles are wrought in the name of Christ."[10]

Professor Peter Brown wrote in his book *Augustine of Hippo* that Augustine carefully collected the evidence of a variety of supernatural incidents and miracles "until they formed a single corpus, as compact and compelling as the miracles that had assisted the growth of the Early Church."[11] For example,

Augustine reported on a person healed of blindness, "The miracle which was wrought at Milan when I was there, and by which a blind man was restored to sight, could come to the knowledge of many; for not only is the city a large one, but also the emperor was there at the time, and the occurrence was witnessed by an immense concourse of people."[12]

The Venerable Bede

The great early English Church leader known as the Venerable Bede, the father of English history, quoted a letter sent by Gregory the Great, the bishop of Rome, in A.D. 601 to Augustine of Canterbury, a missionary sent from Rome to England. Gregory acknowledges the fact that miracles were occurring and that they were very effective in drawing the English natives to faith in Christ: "I know, most loving brother, that Almighty God, by means of your affection, shows great miracles in the nation which he has chosen. Wherefore it is necessary that you rejoice with fear, and tremble whilst you rejoice, on account of the same heavenly gift; viz., that you may rejoice because the souls of the English

Peter Raises Dorcas from Death. Painting by Eustache Le Sueur.

are by outward miracles drawn to inward grace."[13] Gregory also acknowledged in his letter that Augustine personally had "received the gift of working miracles."[14]

Continued Supernatural Miracles

If space permitted, I could quote from a variety of Church authorities over the centuries that followed who witnessed the continued operation of supernatural miracles. These other sources include the famous Bernard of Clairvaux (A.D. 1190–1153) and Martin Luther (A.D. 1483–1546). In addition, there is overwhelming evidence of supernatural miracles that have occurred during the last few centuries during the Welsh Revival and remarkable healings and other miracles witnessed by many reliable sources in the tremendous growth of the Church around the world in the last few decades.

There are many scriptural promises of Jesus Christ regarding His continued supernatural empowering of the Church through His Holy Spirit. "For the Father loveth the Son, and showeth him all things that himself doeth: and he will show him greater works than these, that ye may marvel" (John 5:20). Jesus promised that His faithful followers would be able to do "greater works" because He was empowering the Church with His Holy Spirit. "Verily, verily, I say unto you, He that believeth on me, the works that I do shall he do also; and greater works than these shall he do; because I go unto my Father" (John 14:12).

In addition, the Scripture declared, "For I am the Lord, I change not" (Malachi 3:6). Since God does not, and cannot change His nature, it is consistent and logical to believe that He would continue to manifest His supernatural power of miracles among His people from time to time to demonstrate His continued divine nature and mercy to humanity. Therefore, it is not surprising that our generation, which has witnessed the fulfillment of more remarkable prophecies than any other generation in history, should also witness extraordinary supernatural displays of God's providence, including miracles of healing.

Notes

1. *The Didache* 11:10-11. *Ante-Nicene Library* 10 vols. (Grand Rapids: Wm. B. Eerdmans Publishing Co., 1987).
2. Clement, *Letter to the Corinthians* 2:2. *Ante-Nicene Library* 10 vols. (Grand Rapids: Wm. B. Eerdmans Publishing Co., 1987).
3. *Shepherd of Hermas* 43:9. *Ante-Nicene Library* 10 vols. (Grand Rapids: Wm. B. Eerdmans Publishing Co., 1987).
4. Irenaeus, *Refutation and Overthrow of Knowledge Falsely So Called, Ante-Nicene Library* 10 vols. (Grand Rapids: Wm. B. Eerdmans Publishing Co., 1987).
5. Irenaeus, *Against Heresies* 5:6:1, *Ante-Nicene Library* 10 vols. (Grand Rapids: Wm. B. Eerdmans Publishing Co., 1987).
6. Justin Martyr, *Dialogue with Trypho*, chapter XXXIX. *Ante-Nicene Library* 10 vols. (Grand Rapids: Wm. B. Eerdmans Publishing Co., 1987).
7. Origen, *Against Celsus*, Book I, Chap. XLVI, 2, 8. *Post-Nicene Library* 10 vols. (Grand Rapids: Wm. B. Eerdmans Publishing Co., 1987).
8. Origen, *Against Celsus*, Book VII, Chapter. VIII. *Post-Nicene Library* 10 vols. (Grand Rapids: Wm. B. Eerdmans Publishing Co., 1987).
9. Novatian, *A Treatise of Novatian Concerning the Trinity*, Chapter XXIX, section 251. *Post-Nicene Library* 10 vols. (Grand Rapids: Wm. B. Eerdmans Publishing Co., 1987).
10. Augustine, *The City of God*, Book 22, Chapter 8. *Post-Nicene Library* 10 vols. (Grand Rapids: Wm. B. Eerdmans Publishing Co., 1987).
11. Peter Brown, *Augustine of Hippo* (Berkeley: University of California Press, 1967) 415.
12. Augustine, *The City of God*, Book 22, Chapter 8. *Post-Nicene Library* 10 vols. (Grand Rapids: Wm. B. Eerdmans Publishing Co., 1987).
13. The Venerable Bede, *Ecclesiastical History of England*, Chapter 31, trans. J. A. Giles (London: George Bell & Sons, 1900) 57.
14. The Venerable Bede, *Ecclesiastical History of England*, Chapter 31, trans. J. A. Giles (London: George Bell & Sons, 1900) 57.

26

Why Do Christians Worship on Sunday?

Of all the mysteries that I have been asked about over the years, the question of whether Christians should worship on Sunday or on Saturday has perplexed and bothered more believers than any other question in my experience. It is very unfortunate that so few people know the truth about the question of Sunday versus Saturday worship. I hope that this section will finally answer this important question for many interested people, including pastors and teachers.

Many Christians have been puzzled when asked to explain why the Church worships God on Sunday, the first day of the week, and not on the seventh day of the week, Saturday, the ancient Sabbath day of the Jews. The Bible clearly describes God's command to the Jews to worship Him on the Sabbath, the seventh day of the week, Saturday:

> Remember the sabbath day, to keep it holy. Six days shalt thou labour, and do all thy work: But the seventh day is the sabbath of the Lord thy God: in it thou shalt not

do any work, thou, nor thy son, nor thy daughter, thy manservant, nor thy maidservant, nor thy cattle, nor thy stranger that is within thy gates: For in six days the Lord made heaven and earth, the sea, and all that in them is, and rested the seventh day: wherefore the Lord blessed the sabbath day, and hallowed it. (Exodus 20:8–11)

The early Christians began to use the expression the "Lord's Day" during the first century following the birth of the Church to refer to Sunday as our common day of worship. Revelation 1:10 is the only place in Scripture that uses the expression "the Lord's Day." Sunday was usually identified by the phrase "the first day of the week" throughout the New Testament (Matthew 28:1, Luke 24:1, 1 Corinthians 16:2). Outside the New Testament, the expression "the Lord's Day" appears in the early Church document known as Didache (A.D. 100–110), which includes this statement: "On the day of the resurrection of the Lord, that is, the Lord's day, assemble yourselves together." [1] Note that this statement in an early Church document, the Didache (A.D. 110), only eighty years after Christ's resurrection, confirms that Christians worshipped on Sunday, "On the day of the resurrection of the Lord, that is, the Lord's day."

In the centuries following Christ's resurrection, the expression "the Lord's Day" became a common synonym for Sunday, the day of Jesus' resurrection from the grave. The early Church father Ignatius (A.D. 30–107) was a disciple with Polycarp under the spiritual direction of the Apostle John, their bishop. In the non-canonical book the *Epistle of Ignatius to the Magnesians* (approximately A.D. 101), Ignatius twice used the expression "the Lord's Day" as a reference to Sunday as the common day of Christian worship. Ignatius wrote: "After the observance of the Sabbath, let every friend of Christ keep the Lord's Day as a festival, the resurrection-day, the queen and chief of all the days (of the week). Looking forward to this, the prophet declared, 'To the end, for the eighth day,' on which our life both sprang up again, and the victory over death was obtained in Christ.'" [2]

Note that in addition to acknowledging that the "Lord's Day" was Sunday "the resurrection day," Ignatius notes that this weekly worship festival was similar to the Jewish Sabbath but occurs on a different day—Sunday—the Lord's Day.

Did the Early Church Worship on Saturday or Sunday?

Over the last few centuries a variety of groups, including Seventh-Day Adventists and Seventh-Day Baptists, have claimed that Christians have sinfully abandoned the true Saturday worship of God's biblically authorized Sabbath and adopted Sunday worship, thus "changing the times and laws" of God. They claim that God commanded believers to worship on Saturday and never changed that command. Further, they claim that the early Church unanimously worshipped together on the Saturday Sabbath for many decades or even centuries, until Church leaders arbitrarily changed the day of worship to Sunday without any command or authorization from God.

Some anti—Sunday-worship writers have falsely claimed that the Church initially worshipped on the Saturday Sabbath for almost three centuries until it was suddenly changed to Sunday when Emperor Constantine, the head of the Roman Empire, issued a decree in A.D. 321. This claim that the Church worshipped for centuries on Saturday and then abruptly switched to Sunday as a result of Emperor Constantine is false. The controversy over Saturday or Sunday worship has often confused Christians who do not have access to difficult-to-find books that provide accurate details about the history of the early Church. The historical truth is that the Church never "changed" the day of worship from Saturday to Sunday. From the very beginning of the Church, following the resurrection of our Lord Jesus Christ, both Jewish and Gentile Christians celebrated communion together on Sunday.[3]

Emperor Constantine's decree in A.D. 321 was as follows: "On the venerable Day of the Sun let the magistrates and people residing in cities rest, and let all workshops be closed."[4] A careful examination of this decree by Emperor Constantine will confirm that it did not introduce Sunday as the new day of worship. Rather, this decree was simply the earliest example of a "Sunday closing law," similar to the many similar laws passed in past centuries by Christian nations to encourage a day of labor rest for employees on Sunday. Note that there is no reference to changing the day of worship from Saturday to Sunday.

There is not the slightest evidence in this decree that Emperor Constantine changed the day of worship from Sabbath to Sunday. Rather, Emperor Constantine simply created the first Sunday closing law in recognition that many millions of Roman Christians were already worshipping on Sunday, the first day of the week, as they had from the earliest days of the Christian Church. The historical and scriptural evidence is overwhelming that the Christians worshipped on Sunday from the first days following Christ's resurrection.

If any such arbitrary decree from a Roman Emperor had demanded that the Church change its day of worship from Saturday to Sunday millions of Christians would have rebelled and strongly resisted any such arbitrary change in the day of worship. However, there is not the slightest historical evidence that any such change ever occurred, nor is there any evidence regarding the natural overwhelmingly negative response to such an arbitrary decree regarding changing the day of worship from Saturday to Sunday among the millions of Christians throughout Roman Empire, Africa, and Asia. If anyone arbitrarily attempted to change the appointed day of worship for Christians from the Sabbath to Sunday, the historical records would naturally record a massive debate, resistance, and rebellion from many Christians who would resist such an arbitrary change in such an important issue as the day of the week appointed for religious worship. In addition, no decree from a Roman Emperor would have the slightest influence upon the millions of Christians living in Africa and Asia, yet those African and Asian Christians worshipped on Sunday. Remember, these were the Christians who faced martydom in horrible deaths rather than deny their faith in Jesus Christ. It is inconcievable that they would accept a change in the day of worship simply because a Roman emperor demanded it.

The truth is that immediately following Christ's resurrection, His disciples and followers began to worship on Sunday, the first day of the week, because this was the day that Jesus rose from the grave: "Now on the first day of the week Mary

Magdalene went to the tomb" (John 20:1). Significantly, the early Church was also supernaturally empowered by the Holy Spirit on Pentecost Sunday, which occurred on the fiftieth day counting from the Feast of Firstfruits when Christ arose (Leviticus 23: 16 and Acts 2:1). Beginning with the initial Sabbath of Firstfruits, they counted fifty days (seven weeks of seven days plus one day), which ended on the first day of the week, Sunday). Thus, the two most important days initiating the birth of the Christian faith, Christ's resurrection and the coming of the Holy Spirit at Pentecost, both significant events, occurred through God's providence on Sunday rather than on the Saturday Sabbath. The early Christian writer John Chrysostom wrote a commentary on Psalm 119 that declared that Sunday "was called the Lord's Day because the Lord rose from the dead on that day."

Three specific New Testament texts refer to the early Church worshipping on Sunday. The Apostle Paul wrote to the Church at Corinth, referring to Sunday, "the first day of the week," as the normal day of Christian worship: "Now concerning the collection for the saints, as I have given order to the churches of Galatia, even so do ye. Upon *the first day of the week* let every one of you lay by him in store, as God hath prospered him, that there be no gatherings when I come. And when I come, whomsoever ye shall approve by your letters, them will I send to bring your liberality unto Jerusalem" (1 Corinthians 16:1–3).

In another significant passage, Luke wrote about his rejoining Paul at Philippi and the remarkable resurrection of a youth who fell, asleep, to his death from a window ledge during a long meeting. Luke began his account of the supernatural resurrection of the deceased youth as follows: "And upon *the first day of the week*, when the disciples came together to break bread, Paul preached unto them, ready to depart on the morrow; and continued his speech until midnight" (Acts 20:7).

The third New Testament passage that refers to Sunday is found in the Gospel of John. The apostle wrote of Mary Magdalene as the first of Christ's followers to visit His tomb: "*The first day of the week* cometh Mary Magdalene early, when it was yet dark, unto the sepulchre, and seeth the stone taken away from the sepulchre" (John 20:1). He also wrote,

"Then the same day at evening, being *the first day of the week*, when the doors were shut where the disciples were assembled for fear of the Jews, came Jesus and stood in the midst, and saith unto them, Peace be unto you" (John 20:19).

The Apostle John later authored the book of Revelation, where he again wrote about "the first day of the week" as a reference to Sunday. In Revelation he wrote about the Lord's Day in a clear reference to Sunday in light of his other writings: "I was in the Spirit on the Lord's day, and heard behind me a great voice, as of a trumpet" (Revelation 1:10).

Early Christian Writers' References to Sunday Worship

Further evidence regarding the Christian's worship on Sunday from the beginnings of the early Church is found in the writings of other Church fathers. An early commentary on the writings of Irenaeus (A.D. 120–202) confirmed that Christians worshipped on Sunday from the very beginning. "This custom of not bending the knee upon Sunday, is a symbol of the resurrection, through which we have been set free, by the grace of Christ, from sins, and from death, which has been put to death under Him. Now this custom took its rise from apostolic times, as the blessed Irenaeus, the martyr and bishop of Lyons, declares in his treatise *On Easter*, in which he makes mention of Pentecost also; upon which feast we do not bend the knee, because it is of equal significance with the Lord's day, for the reason already alleged concerning it."[5]

The writer Jerome (A.D. 342–420) noted that Christians worshipped on Sunday. "If it is called day of the Sun by the pagans, we most willingly acknowledge it is as such, since it is on this day that light of the world has appeared and on this day the Son of Justice has risen."[6]

Why Did Jewish Christians Worship on Both Days?

During the first century, historical evidence confirms that many Jewish Christians continued to worship on the Saturday Sabbath because Christ and His disciples never instructed Jews to cease this biblically authorized practice for Jews from the Torah. However, evidence confirms that from the beginning Jewish believers joined with their Gentile Christian brothers in worshipping at the Lord's Supper on Sunday, the day of Christ's resurrection. In other words, many Jewish Christians worshipped on both Saturday and Sunday. Many Church writers noted the difference between the Jewish Sabbath worship and the Christian's Lord's Day on Sunday. An early Church writer, Theodoret, wrote about the heretical Jewish Christian group called Ebonites, who worshipped on both Saturday and Sunday. Theodoret claimed, "They keep the Sabbath according to the Jewish law and sanctify the Lord's Day in like manner as we do."[7]

When Gentiles became Christians, they never began to worship on the Saturday Sabbath of the Jews. They simply began to worship on Sunday, the day of Christ's resurrection and the day of Pentecost.

God's Demand for Worship by Gentile Christians

Although many Jewish Christians naturally continued to observe the Saturday Sabbath in addition to their Sunday worship of communion with Gentile believers, some Jews ceased to worship in the synagogue on Saturday Sabbath. It is significant that God and the Church never commanded Gentile Christians to worship on the Saturday Sabbath. When the issue arose in the Council of the Jerusalem church regarding what spiritual demands should be made on Gentile believers, Luke recorded in the book of Acts the supernaturally inspired decision of the Council of the Jerusalem Church: "For it seemed good to the Holy Ghost, and to us, to lay upon you no greater burden than these necessary things; that you abstain from meats offered to idols, and from blood, and from things strangled, and from fornication: from which if ye keep yourselves, ye shall do well, Fare ye well" (Acts 15:28–29).

The demands upon the Gentile Christians were limited to only four commands: (1) abstain from things polluted by idols; (2) abstain from blood; (3) abstain from things strangled; and (4) abstain from sexual immorality. In these instructions to Gentile converts, note that there was no requirement for Gentile followers of Christ to begin to follow the Old Testament Jewish Law regarding Saturday Sabbath worship.

As more and more Gentiles throughout the Roman Empire became Christians, the Church increasingly became dominated by Gentiles. Gradually, the number of Jewish Christians who observed both Saturday and Sunday dwindled. Finally, after the A.D. 135 Bar Kochba Rebellion, when the Jews in Israel attempted to overthrow their Roman oppressors for the last time, the Jewish Christians were no longer accepted as legitimate Jews by the non-Christian Jews. Fewer and fewer Jews became believers who followed Jesus Christ, until the Church finally became 99 percent Gentile by the end of the first two centuries.

Since God never placed the Gentile Christians under the Sabbath Day obligation of the Mosaic Law, they naturally continued to worship Christ on Sunday as they had from the beginning. The changing demographic balance between Jewish believers and Gentile believers within the Church eventually resulted in a primarily Gentile Christian Church that worshipped solely on Sunday.

Why Do Some Desire to Observe the Saturday Sabbath?

The Seventh-Day Adventists and several other groups suggest that the abandonment of the Saturday Sabbath worship was the great sin of the Antichrist system, "the changing of times and laws" prophesied to occur in the last days. This claim is a blatant appeal to spiritual pride to return to the system of religious law that proved to be such an impossible spiritual burden for Israel. The commandment for the observance of a Saturday Sabbath was given to Israel. It was never given as a direct commandment to the Gentiles, nor was it given to the Church.

The Apostle Paul addressed the Galatian church on this very same issue of whether Christians should attempt to follow the old Jewish Law or place their entire hope of salvation in faith in Jesus Christ. "Are you so foolish? Having begun in the Spirit, are you now being made perfect by the flesh?" (Galatians 3:3). We can never succeed in obeying the law 100 percent and, therefore, we can never please God by total obedience to the Old Testament Law. The purpose of the Law was to teach us, as a "schoolmaster," that we could never meet the mark of perfect obedience to God's Law. The word *sin* is derived from the term "to miss the mark." Therefore our only hope of salvation lies in our acceptance through faith and personal repentance of the complete atonement for our sins by Christ's sacrificial death on the Cross. The attempt to observe Saturday Sabbath worship, rather than the normal Sunday worship of all Christians for the last two thousand years, is a spiritually misguided attempt to place believers under the impossible and failed Law recorded in the Old Testament rather than relying for our salvation on Christ's offer of salvation through His death on the Cross and entirely unmerited grace—the undeserved gift of God to His children.

Christ Appears to Mary. Painting by G. Aus Der Ohe.

Notes

1. *Didache* 14. *Ante-Nicene Fathers* (Grand Rapids: Wm. B. Eerdmans Publishing Co. 1986).
2. Ignatius, *Epistle of Ignatius to the Magnesians. Ante-Nicene Fathers* (Grand Rapids: Wm. B. Eerdmans Publishing Co. 1986).
3. Ignatius, *Epistle of Ignatius to the Magnesians.* Ante-Nicene Fathers (Grand Rapids: Wm. B. Eerdmans Publishing Co. 1986).
4. Constantine, March 7, 321. Codex Justinianus lib. 3, tit. 12, 3. In Philip Schaff, *History of the Christian Church,* Vol. 3. 380.
5. Irenaeus, *Fragments from Lost Writings of Irenaeus—Ante-Nicene Fathers,* (Grand Rapids: Wm. B. Eerdmans Publishing Co. 1986).
6. Jerome, *In die dominica Paschae homilia,* CCL 78, 550, 1, 52. *Ante-Nicene Fathers* (Grand Rapids: Wm. B. Eerdmans Publishing Co. 1986).
7. Theodoret, *Fab. Haeret.* 2:1. *Ante-Nicene Fathers* (Grand Rapids: Wm. B. Eerdmans Publishing Co. 1986).

27

The Final Mystery: Salvation through Jesus Christ

The greatest mystery of all is the mystery of God's plan of salvation for all those who place their faith and trust in Jesus Christ. The apostle Paul wrote to his disciple Timothy and pointed out the importance of the "mystery of godliness" that reveals God's plan to save all sinners who look to Jesus for salvation. "And without controversy great is the mystery of godliness: God was manifest in the flesh, justified in the Spirit, seen of angels, preached unto the Gentiles, believed on in the world, received up into glory" (1 Timothy 3:16).

Paul wrote to the Colossians and reminded them that the mystery of salvation through Jesus Christ was now available to both the Jews and the Gentiles. "Even the mystery which hath been hid from ages and from generations, but now is made manifest to his saints: To whom God would make known what is the riches of the glory of this mystery among the Gentiles;

which is Christ in you, the hope of glory" (Colossians 1:26–27). This profound mystery of God's plan to redeem sinners from the curse and punishment of sin, which had been hidden from the very beginning of humanity, was finally revealed in the life, death, and resurrection of Christ.

The apostle Paul received a divine revelation that God "commandeth all men every where to repent: because he hath appointed a day, in the which he will judge the world in righteousness by that man whom he hath ordained; whereof he hath given assurance unto all men, in that he hath raised him from the dead" (Acts 17:30–31).

Every one of us will someday stand face to face before Jesus Christ as our God and Judge. We will all have to give an account of the decision we have made regarding our relationship with Him. Every one of us has rebelled against God and sinned throughout our life. The apostle Paul wrote, "For all have sinned, and come short of the glory of God" (Romans 3:23). The consequence of our choice to sinfully rebel against God is that we have all walked away from God's holy presence and have thus become unfit to enter a sinless and holy heaven. God's Word declares, "For the wages of sin is death; but the gift of God is eternal life through Jesus Christ our Lord" (Romans 6:23). The Scriptures declare that our sinful rebellion has alienated each of us from the holiness of God. Our continued rebellion and rejection of Christ will prevent us from ever entering heaven until our sins are forgiven. The sacrificial death of Jesus Christ on the Cross is the only hope to bring us to a place of true peace in our soul. The death of our old sinful nature when we identify with Christ's death on the Cross will open the door to finding true peace with God.

At the end of His life and ministry, Jesus asked His disciples this vital question that we all must answer: "'But whom say ye that I am? And Simon Peter answered and said, Thou art the Christ, the Son of the living God'" (Matthew 16:15–16). Every one of us must answer that ultimate question for ourselves. If the Bible is truly the Word of God, then our answer to that question about faith in Jesus will determine our eternal destiny. We cannot evade our responsibility to answer this question about Jesus Christ. If we refuse to answer, we have already rejected

Christ's claims to be our Savior and Lord. Then we will face the consequences of our rejection of God's only plan of salvation.

Paul wrote, "For it is written, As I live, saith the Lord, every knee shall bow to me, and every tongue shall confess to God. So then every one of us shall give account of himself to God" (Romans 14:11–12). The Scriptures declare that someday every one of us will spiritually bow our knee to Jesus Christ and acknowledge Him as Almighty God. "That at the name of Jesus every knee should bow, of things in heaven, and things in earth, and things under the earth" (Philippians 2:10). The question is: Will you choose to repent of your sins now and bow your knee joyfully to your Savior and Lord? Or, will you reject His offer of salvation today and finally be forced by His majesty to bow your knee before your final Judge as you are sent to an eternity in hell?

On Judgment Day when all of us meet Jesus Christ, everyone will know whether we personally accepted or rejected His precious offer of salvation. When Jesus was crucified on the Cross, He paid the complete and final price for our sins. Jesus' final statement on the Cross was, "It is finished." As the sinless Lamb of God, Jesus allowed Himself to be offered as a perfect sacrifice to pay the price of our sins and to reconcile each of us to God. However, in a similar manner as a pardon is sometimes offered to a prisoner awaiting execution, each of us must personally repent of our sins and accept Christ's pardon for His gift of salvation to become effective. The basis of God's judgment following our death will be our personal relationship with Jesus Christ—not whether we were better or worse than most other people. Our relationship with Christ will determine whether we will spend our eternity with God in heaven or an eternity without Him in hell.

Some suggest that if God is truly a God of love, then somehow He will be "kind" and bend the rules to allow "good" people into heaven despite their lifelong rejection of Christ's gift of salvation. Consider the implications of this proposition for a moment. If God allowed sinners who refused to repent of their sins into heaven, He would have to deny His nature as a holy and just God. Admitting unrepentant sinners into heaven would transform Paradise into a spiritual annex of hell.

If an unrepentant soul were allowed into heaven, his sinfulness would destroy the holiness of heaven. In addition, an unrepentant sinner would hate the holiness of heaven and would despise the constant worship of God. The sinless nature of a holy heaven and the evil nature of sin make it absolutely impossible for God to forgive men's sins unless they wholeheartedly repent and turn from sinful rebellion. Only then can God forgive us and transform us into one saved by the grace of Jesus Christ, who cleanses us from our sinful rebellion. Although we can cleanse our bodies with water, the cleansing of our souls requires the spiritual application of the blood of Christ to our hearts to prepare us to live in a holy heaven.

Nicodemus was one of the most important righteous religious leaders of ancient Israel. He privately came to Jesus at night and questioned Him about how he could be saved. Jesus answered, "Verily, verily, I say unto thee, Except a man be born again, he cannot see the kingdom of God" (John 3:3). It isn't simply a matter of intellectually accepting the facts about Christ and salvation. To be "born again," we must sincerely repent of our sinful rebellion, asking Jesus to forgive us and to wholeheartedly trust in Christ for the rest of our life. This spiritual decision will transform us forever. God will give us a new purpose and meaning to our life. The Lord promises believers eternal life in heaven: "This is the will of Him who sent Me, that everyone who sees the Son and believes in Him may have everlasting life; and I will raise him up at the last day" (John 6:40). The moment you commit your life to Christ, you will receive the promise of eternal life. Though your body will someday die, you will live forever with Christ in heaven. Jesus explained to Nicodemus, "For God so loved the world, that he gave his only begotten Son, that whosoever believeth in him should not perish, but have everlasting life" (John 3:16).

Every sinner stands condemned by God because of his lifelong sinful rebellion against God's commandments as revealed in the Scriptures. Jesus Christ warned, "He that believeth in him is not condemned: but he that believeth not is condemned already, because he hath not believed in the name of the only begotten Son of God" (John 3:18). After forty years of studying the greatest mysteries of the Bible, I am convinced that it is the inspired Word of God. Therefore, I believe the words of Jesus Christ, "I am the way, the truth, and the life: no man cometh unto the Father, but by me" (John 14:6). God declares in these inspired words that there is no other road to salvation other than accepting the "way," the "truth" and the "life" of Jesus Christ.

Christ's sacrificial gift of His life on the Cross paid the price for our sins, purchasing our salvation through His great sacrifice. Every one of us, by personally accepting Christ's pardon, will now be able to stand before the Judgment Seat of God clothed in Christ's righteousness: "For he hath made him [Jesus] to be sin for us, who knew no sin; that we might be made the righteousness of God in him" (2 Corinthians 5:21). Christ's atonement for our sins is perhaps the greatest mystery in creation. Jesus is the only one in history who, by His sinless life, was personally qualified to enter heaven by His own obedience and righteousness. Yet the mystery of salvation is that He loved each of us so much that He chose to die upon that Cross to purchase our salvation. In a marvelous act of God's mercy, the innocent righteousness of Jesus is placed to our account with God.

The greatest mystery of all is that Jesus Christ, the sinless Son of God, took upon Himself all of the terrible sins and evil of humanity when He hung upon the Cross as the perfect sacrifice for our salvation. In a mystery beyond our human understanding, Jesus Christ somehow became sin for us so that we, by accepting His sacrificial gift through faith in Him, can become the righteousness of Christ and thereby qualify to enter heaven. Only those who are pure and holy may enter heaven. When we accept Jesus Christ's sacrifice on the Cross in payment for our sinful rebellion, the innocence and holiness of Christ is placed to our account before God so that He no longer sees our sinful rebellion; rather, He sees the righteousness of His holy Son, Jesus Christ. The Lord then calls us to enter into His holy heaven, "Come, ye blessed of my Father, inherit the kingdom prepared for you from the foundation of the world" (Matthew 25:34).

The mystery is that all that God requires of us to enable Jesus Christ to become our personal Savior from the guilt of sin is that we turn from our sin and pride in true repentance. The apostle John wrote, "But as many as received him, to them gave he power to become sons of God, even to them that believe on his name" (John 1:12). Your decision will change your eternal destiny, but it will also give you peace today as your guilt from sin will be removed forever.

Your decision to accept Christ as your personal Savior is the most important one you will ever make. It will cost you a great deal to live as a committed Christian in our immoral and anti-Christian world today. Many will challenge your new faith in the salvation of your soul through Jesus Christ. The British writer John Stuart Mill wrote about the importance of our belief in Christ and the tremendous influence a believer can have on those around them: "One person with a belief is equal to ninety-nine people who only have opinions."

Jesus Christ commands His disciples, "Follow Me." Your decision and commitment to Christ will transform your life forever. Your commitment to Christ will allow His divine grace and supernatural power to transform your life into one of joy and spiritual peace. While your commitment to follow Christ will cost you a great deal, your decision to reject Christ's offer of salvation will cost you everything when you die. Jesus challenges us to carefully consider the importance of our decision with these words, "For what shall it profit a man, if he shall gain the whole world, and lose his own soul?" (Mark 8:36).

If you are ready to place your faith and trust in Jesus Christ, I encourage you to pray this prayer sincerely:

> Lord God, I know that I have been a rebel and sinner against you all of my life. I accept that Jesus Christ died for my sins and I now accept Him as my Lord and Savior. I repent of my sinful rebellion and ask Christ to forgive me and transform me so that I may follow Him faithfully. Lord, make me a faithful Christian, ready to worship and serve you. Give me the courage to share my new faith with others.

Selected Bibliography

Anderson, Robert, *Human Destiny*. London: Pickering & Inglish, 1913.

Aviezer, Nathan, *In The Beginning . . . Biblical Creation and Science*. Hoboken: KTAV Publishing House, Inc., 1990.

Ball, C. J., *Light From The East*. London: Eyre and Spottiswoode, 1899.

Bentwich, Norman, *Fulfilment in the Promised Land*. London: The Soncino Press, 1938.

Blomberg, Craig, *The Historical Reliability of the Gospels*. Leicester: Inter-Varsity Press, 1987.

Blunt, Rev. J. J., *Undesigned Coincidences in the Old and New Testament*. London: John Murray, 1876.

Bright, John, *The Authority of the Old Testament*. Grand Rapids: Baker Book House, 1967.

Burrows, Millar, *The Dead Sea Scrolls of St. Marks Monastery*. New Haven: The American Schools of Oriental Research, 1950.

Cobern, Camden M., *The New Archeological Discoveries*. London: Funk & Wagnalls Co., 1929.

Duncan, J. Garrow, *Digging Up Biblical History*, Vol. I & II. London: Society For Promoting Christian Knowledge, 1931.

Finegan, Jack, *Light From the Ancient Past*. Princeton: Princeton University Press, 1946.

Finegan, Jack, *Archeological History of the Ancient Middle East*. New York: Dorsett Press, 1979.

Flavius, Josephus, *Antiquities of the Jews*. Grand Rapids: Kregal Publications, 1960.

Frazer, Sir James George, *Folk-Lore in the Old Testament*. London: Macmillan and Co., Limited., 1919.

Gaussen, L., *The Divine Inspiration of the Bible*. Grand Rapids: Kregel Publications, 1971.

Geikie, Cunningham, *The Holy Land and the Bible*. New York: James Pott & Co. Publishers, 1891.

Keith, Alexander, *Christian Evidences: Fulfilled Bible Prophecy*. Minneapolis: Klock & Klock Christian Publishers, Inc., 1984.

Kenyon, Frederic, *The Bible and Archeology*. London: George G. Harrap & Co. Ltd., 1940.

Kenyon, Frederic, *The Story of the Bible*. London: John Murray, 1936.

Kenyon, Frederic, *Our Bible and the Ancient Manuscripts*. London: Eyre & Spottiswoode, 1948.

Layard, Austen H., *Discoveries Among the Ruins of Nineveh and Babylon*. New York: Harper & Brothers, 1853.

Little, Paul, *Know Why You Believe*. Downers Grove: Inter-Varsity Press, 1988.

Loftus, William Kennett, *Travels and Researches in Chaldea and Susiana*. London: James Nisbet & Co., 1857.

Maspero, Gaston, *History of Egypt*. London: The Grolier Society, 1900.

McDowell, Josh, *Evidence That Demands a Verdict*. Arrowhead Springs: Campus Crusade For Christ, 1972.

Morris, Henry M., *Many Infallible Proofs*. El Cajun: Master Books, 1974.

Morris, Henry M., *The Bible and Modern Science*. Chicago: Moody Press, 1968.

Morris, Henry M., *The Biblical Basis for Modern Science*. Grand Rapids: Baker Book House, 1984.

Morris, Henry M., *Scientific Creationism*. El Cajon: Master Books, 1985.

Morris, Herbert W., *Testimony of the Ages*. St. Louis: William Garretson & Co., 1884.

Ragozin, Zenaide A., *Chaldea from the Earliest Times to the Rise of Assyria*. London: T. Fisher Unwin, 1886.

Rappaport, S., *History of Egypt*. London: The Grolier Society, 1904.

Rawlinson, George, *History of Herodutus*, 4 vol. London: John Murray, 1875.

Robertson, A. T., *Luke the Historian in the Light of Research*. New York: Charles Scribner's Sons, 1923.

Robinson, John A. T., *Redating the New Testament*. Philadelphia: The Westminster Press, 1976.

Robinson, Gershon, *The Obvious Proof*. London: CIS Publishers, 1993.

Rule, William Harris, *Biblical Monuments*. Croydon: Werteimer, Lea and Co., 1873.

Sayce, A. H., *Records of the Past*, 5 vol. London: Samuel Bagster & Sons, Ltd., 1889.

Siculus, Diodorus, *Library of History*. Cambridge: Harvard University Press, 1989.

Smith, George Adam, *The Historical Geography of the Holy Land*. London: Hodder and Stoughton, 1894.

Stanley, Arthur Penrhyn, *Sinai and Palestine*. London: John Murray, 1905.

Thompson, J. A., *The Bible and Archeology*. Grand Rapids: Eerdmans Publishing Co. 1972.

Thompson, William M., *The Land and the Book*. Hartford: The S. S. Scranton Co., 1910.

Tiffany, Osmond, *Sacred Biography and History*. Chicago: Hugh Heron, 1874.

Unger, Merrill, F., *Archeology and the Old Testament*. Grand Rapids: Zondervan Publishing Co., 1954.

Vermes, Geza, *The Dead Sea Scrolls In English*. London: Penguin Books, 1988.

Vermes, Geza, *Discovery in the Judean Desert*. New York: Desclee Co., 1956.

Vincent, J. H., *Curiosities of the Bible*. Chicago: R. C. Treat., 1885.

Vos, Howard, *Can I Trust The Bible?* Chicago: Moody Press, 1963.

Warfield, Benjamin Breckinridge, *The Inspiration and Authority of the Bible*. Philadelphia: The Presbyterian and Reformed Publishing Company, 1970.

Wilson, Bill, *A Ready Defense — The Best of Josh McDowell*. San Bernardino: Here's Life Publishers, Inc., 1990.

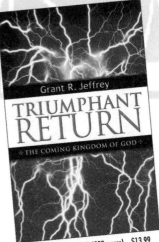

ISBN #0-921714-60-2 (288 pages) $13.99

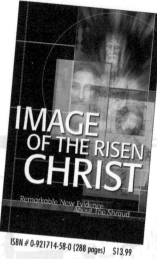

ISBN # 0-921714-58-0 (288 pages) $13.99

From

FRONTIER RESEARCH
P U B L I C A T I O N S · I N C

BESTSELLING TITLES

ISBN # 0-967009-80-4 (320 pages) $12.99

ISBN # 0-921714-56-4 (288 pages) $13.99

AVAILABLE IN CHRISTIAN BOOKSTORES EVERYWHERE
(OR BY CALLING) IN USA: 1-800-883-1812   IN CANADA: 1-800-853-1423

(Prices may vary in Canada)

Frontier Research Publications

Grant Jeffrey Ministries

FRONTIER RESEARCH PUBLICATIONS·INC

Available in Christian bookstores everywhere

Quantity	Code	Description		Price	Total
		Softback Books			
	BK-3	Messiah – War in the Middle East & The Road to Armageddon		$12.99	
	BK-4	Apocalypse – The Coming Judgment of the Nations		$12.99	
	BK-5	Prince of Darkness – Antichrist and the New World Order		$13.99	
	BK-6	Final Warning – Economic Collapse and Coming World Government		$13.99	
	BK-7	Heaven – The Mystery of Angels		$12.99	
	BK-9	Yeshua – The Name of Jesus Revealed in the Old Testament (Yacov Rambsel)		$11.99	
	BK-10	Armageddon – Appointment With Destiny		$12.99	
	BK-11	His Name is Jesus – The Mysterious Yeshua Codes (Yacov Rambsel)		$12.99	
	BK-12	The Handwriting of God – Sacred Mysteries of the Bible		$13.99	
	BK-14	The New World Religion (Gary H. Kah)		$12.99	
	BK-16	Jesus, The Great Debate		$13.99	
	BK-17	Image of the Risen Christ (Dr. Kenneth E. Stevenson)		$13.99	
	BK-18	Surveillance Society – The Rise of Antichrist		$13.99	
	BK-19	Journey Into Eternity – Search for Immortality		$13.99	
	BK-20	Triumphant Return – The Coming Kingdom of God		$13.99	
	BK-21	The War on Terror – Unfolding Bible Prophecy		$12.99	
	BK-22	The Signature of God (Expanded and Revised)		$13.99	
	BK-23	Unveiling Mysteries of the Bible		$12.99	
		ANY THREE BOOKS OR MORE	**EACH**	**$11.00**	
		Hardcover Books			
	HC-H	Heaven – The Mystery of Angels		$15.99	
	W-50	Mysterious Bible Codes		$29.99	
	W-51	Flee The Darkness (Grant R. Jeffrey and Angela Hunt)	*Fiction*	$27.99	
	W-52	By Dawn's Early Light (Grant R. Jeffrey and Angela Hunt)	*Fiction*	$27.99	
	W-53	The Spear of Tyranny (Grant R. Jeffrey and Angela Hunt)	*Fiction*	$19.99	
		Videos			
	V-20	Jesus, The Great Debate		$19.99	
	V-22	The War on Terror – Unfolding Bible Prophecy		$19.99	
		Double-length Videos			
	V-17	The Signature of God – Astonishing Biblical Discoveries		$29.99	
	V-18	Mysterious Bible Codes		$29.99	
	VP-1	Final Warning – Big Brother Government		$29.99	
		Total this page (to be carried forward)			

continued overleaf

Quantity	Code	Description	Price	Total
			Total from previous page	
		Audio Cassettes		
	AB-14	The Signature of God (2 tapes)	$15.99	
	AB-15	Mysterious Bible Codes (2 tapes)	$15.99	
	AB-17	Jesus, The Great Debate (2 tapes)	$15.99	
		Computer Programs		
	BC	Bible Codes 2000 (on CD-ROM; for IBM-compatible computers only)	$44.99	
	PIB	**Product Brochure**	No charge	
		One low shipping and handling fee for the above (per order)	$4.95	$4.95
		Jeffrey Prophecy Study Bible		
	KJV	Hardcover	$34.99	
	KJV	Bonded Leather: Black	$59.99	
	KJV	Bonded Leather: Burgundy	$59.99	
	NIV	Hardcover	$34.99	
	NIV	Bonded Leather: Black	$59.99	
	NIV	Bonded Leather: Burgundy	$59.99	
		Shipping and handling fee for Bibles (per order)	$5.95	$5.95
		Oklahoma residents add 7.5% sales tax		

Additional shipping charges will apply to orders outside North America.   **Grand Total**

All prices are in U.S. dollars

U.S. orders: mail along with your check or money order to:
Frontier Research Publications
P.O. Box 470470
Tulsa, OK 74147-0470

**Canadian orders:
call or write for pricing to:**
Frontier Research Publications
P.O. Box 129, Station "U", Toronto,
Ontario M8Z 5M4

U.S. credit card orders:
           call 1-800-883-1812

Canadian credit card orders:
           call 1-800-853-1423

Prices effective July 1, 2002